Cooking

a Fairytale

400
RECIPES AND IDEAS
FOR CHILDREN'S PARTIES
BY

ALEXIA ALEXIADOU

Recipes / Texts: Alexia Alexiadou

Food Styling: Alexia Alexiadou

Published by: Alba Editions

Art direction: Laura Venizelou

Photographs: Viviana Athanassopoulou

Styling: Viviana Athanassopoulou, Laura Venizelou

Translation: Litterae

Films: Orion Prepress Studio

Printed by: E. Daniil & Co S.A.

Bookbinder: Dionyssis Dedes

ISBN: 960-85875-1-4

Copyright© 2004 Alexia Alexiadou

13, Lykovrisseos & Iroon Polytechniou St., 141 23 Lykovrissi

Tel.: 210 28.56.057 – 62, Fax: 210 28.13.455

www.bestcookbooks.gr, e-mail: aalexiadou@albaeditions.gr

1st edition: May 2004

Acknowledgements

Warm thanks to Mrs Thalia Sotiriadou for offering her house in Kefalari where the photographs for the "Christmas Surprise" chapter were taken.

Many thanks to the following stores, which provided photo props:

Vefa's House, 1, Kressnas St., Lykovrissi, tel.: 210 28 46 984, e-mail: info@vefashouse.gr, www.vefashouse.gr
Habitat, 250-254 Kifissias Ave., Halandri, tel.: 210 67 78 880
Frattina, 127, Harilaou Trikoupi St., N. Erythrea, tel.: 210 80 79 329
Utopia, 26, Skoufa St., Kolonaki, tel.: 210 36 12 179
www.home.com, 16, Levidou St., and 1-3 Argyropoulou St., Kifissia, tel.: 210 62 33 520

I am grateful to Christina Brousali for photographing the children for the "Birthday party at the summer house" chapter, at Vefa Alexiadou's house in Halkidiki. Finally, many many thanks to the amazing little "stars" and "starlets" of this book, who gave its pages all their joy, vitality and joie de vivre:

Marilyn Achoyin, Spyros Antonatos, Vivianne Argyriadou, Lydia Assimakopoulou, Matina Assimakopoulou, Freddy Barouch, Giorgos Biniaris, Alexis Christellis, Tino Christellis, Cecilia Chroneou, Marilena Douka, Konstantinos Doukas, Katerina Giamarellou, Sonya Giamarellou, Giannis Gonidakis, Konstantinos Gonidakis, Avgoustinos Hajipanis, Evgenia Kanata, Katerina Kapagiannidou, Daphne Kassimati, Filippos Kassimatis, Nefeli Katsou, Filippos Kiourtsidakis, Lefteris Kiourtsidakis, Hara Kitsaki, Fanis Maratsinos, Alexandra Maridi, Daphne Maridi, Nefeli Mina, Danae Panagopoulou, Vivianne Perrou, Marky Pertsemlidi, Maria Pramantioti, Alexandros Psalidopoulos, Natalie Psomiadou, Panos Rasias, Anastasia Siati, Marina Siati, Anna Stroutsi, Myrsini Stroutsi, Panagiotis Stroutsis, Myrto Touloupi, Kate Voutsina and Eftychia Zaragga

Alexia Alexiadou's first book, Exotic Cuisine, was published in 1996. Exotic Cuisine was the author's first complete work after several years of experience in the culinary world. It is the result of a new but successful career, which brought her from the world of finance and an MBA from City University of London, to her great passion, which due to tradition could be no other than cooking.

Alexia Alexiadou jointly with her mother, Vefa Alexiadou has appeared daily for many years in the most popular morning show of Greek television. In co-operation with her mother, she has published many cookbooks; most of them best sellers in Greece and abroad. The book "Sunny Mediterranean Cuisine" which contains a great collection of healthy vegan and seafood recipes, has received an award in the French culinary capital, Perigueux in 1999 as well as the silver medal for its photography at the Jacob's Creek Awards, in Australia the same year.

Alexia Alexiadou's book "Cooking a love affair", which established her as one of the most successful representatives of creative Greek cuisine, was released on February 14th, 2001 and also received an award in France during the same year.

Alexia Alexiadou's book, "Wedding Days", received an award in Perigueux, France, in 2002, as the best Entertaining book in Greece. "Cooking a Fairytale" has won an international award in the same competition for Best Cover as well as Best Greek Children's cookook and has been nominated for Best Children's Cookbook in the world for the year 2004. Her latest book is Exotic Cuisine, a re-launch of her first best-seller in an updated modernized version, which will soon be available in English.

Alexia Alexiadou was born in Thessalonica and lives permanently in Athens with her husband and their two precious daughters. Alexia and her husband Evangelos Kitsakis jointly own Alba Editions, whose aim is to offer luxurious coffee-table, lifestyle cookbooks to the demanding lovers of the culinary arts.

The happy outcome of "love and marriage" is the miraculous creation of a new life. Ten little fingers, two little feet, one big smile and the pattering around the house are what really fill our lives and hearts with happiness. With a lot of respect for those who appreciate the value of the family, I present to you "Cooking a Fairytale" the last book of the culinary trilogy begun by the award-winning "Cooking a love affair" and the also award-winning "Wedding Days".

Prepared with special love at a period in my life when my firstborn daughter Hara drew all my attention at the tender preschool age, this book brought me extra blessings, more than I could have wished for, as at its final stage I heard the happy news; my second baby was on the way! The release of this book coincided with the birth of my second daughter Genova and the feeling is overwhelming...

Creating this book was a fun-filled experience, watching happy faces running around the studio all day long, munching away at all the muffins, cookies and cakes prepared by them, my sweet little chefs! I wish to dedicate this book to all the children of the world, the strong foundations of the future, who look to us, their parents, for guidance, creative companionship and traditional values. Like blank pages, their little minds await for us to draw beautiful and meaningful pictures on them, memories which will later develop into a family tradition that they, in turn, will pass on to the next generation.

Every single day, the "little buds" seek attention and acknowledgment from the adult members of the family. Using their imagination creatively, usually with drawings and quite often by singing and dancing, they try to fill their spare time and elicit admiration from their parents. Teach your children the art of cooking and discover how to spend endless hours of fun with your whole family. The most important thing is to include your children in everyday work in the kitchen, give them responsibilities and roles, so that their time in the house is spent pleasantly and creatively. Invent beautiful things with them; imagine that your kitchen is the stage, a perfect setting for dreaming up a unique fairytale.

Every day can be a celebration, from the simple preparation of a Sunday meal en famille, to baking cookies and cakes for school lunches, to organizing a children's party. The contribution of the youngest members of the family is important, from setting the table to preparing the food. Children can decorate the party room, draw the invitations, bake cookies, create unique sandwiches, and even garnish the most elaborate cake. Children are capable of anything, as long as we trust them.

All my childhood memories are filled with aromas of food, freshly baked cookies and cakes, vanilla and cinnamon, warm caramel and chocolate fudge, bringing to mind the little nursery rhyme "Sugar and spice and all things nice". My favorite working space in our old house was the large oak table in the center of our kitchen. Coming from a family whose work has always been cooking and creating beautiful books, my whole life could not but be tightly entangled with the kitchen and its aromas. No wonder then, that today my kitchen is the most beautiful and spacious room at home. Sweet memories from my childhood fill my mind; all those years when my father and I baked traditional Easter cookies and prepared mayonnaise-based salads for every family gathering. In that same kitchen, my mother and I baked meringues on a weekly basis as this was her favorite dessert, and I still tingle at the memory of the velvety sweetness of beaten egg whites and sugar left over on the whisk. Next to my mother, I learnt everything I can or

dare to claim I know today about my favorite sector, confectionary.

When I was at the age of twelve, my mother wrote her first book on children's parties dedicating it to me and wishing that one day I would write my own book. I believe I was her inspiration as much as today my daughter Hara inspires me. At that age, I cooked and organized my first school party; the first but not the last, because from then on, all my friends' home gatherings became my exclusive responsibility. On school holidays my house was always full of classmates, girls and boys, and our main occupation would be to bake a cake, prepare a Chinese meal or make pancakes and enjoy them with chocolate praline cream. We enjoyed feeling like responsible 'adults', getting a small glimpse of the magic world of grown-ups, while some parents certainly felt happy knowing where we were and what we were doing.

Loving family memories, joyful times with good friends, laughter and creative occupation; that is what cooking has always meant to me, and that is the image of work in the kitchen that has been imprinted in my mind since I was a child. All this has taught me that we should trust children, even the youngest ones, to create works of art in cooking or confectionary. Since she took her first steps, my firstborn daughter has spent her time in the kitchen with me. Her creations, marzipan fruit and vegetables, double-chocolate cup-cakes and cream cheese desserts concocted by her, have been photographed, and I am proud to present them in this book.

First steps are always difficult, so don't despair if the first attempt, especially with preschool-aged children, ends unsuccessfully with a "half" baked dessert and a "totally" dirty kitchen. Spend time consistently with the children, guide them and teach them with patience, show them the right way to work in the kitchen, how to succeed in what they are doing and how to consider tidiness a game, so that they always leave their work space clean and tidy. Children receive numerous messages. In considering work a game, and without realizing it, they learn to be tidy, organized and close to their family. They learn to offer and share, to compete and create, to produce and to perfect. You will achieve all this especially if you invite two or more children to spend time creatively in the kitchen.

Don't wait for Christmas, a special anniversary or someone's birthday to organize a small or large children's gathering. Go through the book together with your children and find more than one opportunity in every season to organize a small or large celebration. Remember that the greatest responsibility is raising your children in the right way, in these hard times when visions, values and ideals are constantly contested, especially by those who do not realize that it is our obligation to form a generation that resists and creates. Give this generation love, warmth and security, and rest assured that it will be returned to you open-handedly in the future.

ALEXIA ALEXIADOU – MAY 2004

"To Hara and Genovefa,
granddaughters and grandmothers"

Parties for all children

Baby first birthday
Dream butterfly party
August party at the country house
Christmas surprise

Parties for pre-school children
Dream butterfly party
Heart party
Dolls' tea party
August birthday at the summer house
"Make food not war" party
Let's bake cookies
Christmas surprise

Parties for primary-school children
Slumber party
Heart party
Dream butterfly party
August birthday at the summer house
Chocolate mania
Party for good witches and wizards
"Make food not war" party
Cake etc...
For your special day Mum

Parties for teenagers
Cakes etc...
For your special day Mum
Valentine's sweetheart party
American dream party
Back to school
Chocolate mania
Halloween party (for good witches...)

Parties for girls only
Dream butterfly party
Heart party
Dolls' tea party
For your special day Mum

Party for boys only
Chocolate mania
Back to school
Christmas surprise
let's play ball party

contents

INTRODUCTION pp. 8-11

1 KITCHEN PARTIES pp. 12-71

Cakes etc...14 Let's bake cookies...30 For your special day, Mommy...38 Slumber party...48 Chocolate mania...62

2 GARDEN PARTIES pp. 72-149

Little fairies' spring party...74 American Dream, pool party or beach party...92 "Make food, not war" hippie party...110 "Let's play ball" picnic in the park...128 August birthday party at the summerhouse...138

3 HOUSE PARTIES pp. 150-233

Back to school...150 Christmas Surprise...164 Valentine's sweetheart party...188 Invitation to my doll's tea party...206 Good witches and little wizards' Halloween party...222

LET'S PARTY SOME MORE   pp. 234-235
GLOSSARY FOR YOUNG CHEFS   p. 236
INDEX   pp. 237-239

On the morning of the party

1. Take out all the things stored in the freezer. Most of the food needs to be defrosted before you can cook it. Fill bowls of nuts or crisps two hours before the party and not before, because they will get soggy.

2. For winter parties, it helps to find somewhere in the house, a room, storage area, garage or covered veranda, which you can use for storage when the refrigerator is full of dishes. Prepare the dishes of canapés, sandwiches or anything else that needs to be refrigerated, cover them with plastic wrap and store them there.

In the afternoon of the party

1. For winter parties, it is a good idea to place the cake in the center of the table at the beginning of the party, making sure that it can be admired by the parents but not touched by the children, so that you can show off the masterpiece you put so much effort into. A homemade cake always tastes better; so don't be convinced by the fancy decorations of store-bought ones. The birthday cake is the highlight of the party, so make its preparation a happy event at which your child can participate.

2. Start baking 1 hour before the party. When all oven-food is cooked, store it in the oven at a very low temperature.

3. Prepare the coffee just before the party starts and arrange the cakes or cookies, milk and sugar, napkins and spoons prettily on a small table in the adult area. In this way, you won't have to look for everything at the last minute when everyone is asking for coffee. Also fill a large jug with cold water and have plenty of glasses to hand, so guests can help themselves.

4. As the guests arrive, keep all the gifts together, so that your child doesn't open them at once. This would disorient the children and take away the birthday boy or girl's enjoyment after the party, when everyone will have left and your child will be feeling a little sad. Lead the children directly to the area prepared for their entertainment.

5. The best time for serving the food is near the middle of the party if it is taking place in the afternoon, and a little later if it is in the morning.

6. Cut the cake before starting on the food, so as to have the full attention of all the guests. Gather the children and adults together in the pre-arranged location. Don't forget everything you need for photographing or filming the party's big moment. Light the candles and sing the birthday song many times, as these are unique moments, the climax of the party you put so much effort into.

7. At eating time, serve the children first, and then the adults. Ask a friend to help you serve out the dishes. Don't try to do everything by yourself, as this will lead to frustration and unnecessary fatigue. Make sure the person or persons employed to entertain the children are aware that they will attend and help with the children's food.

The end of the party

1. If you have any birthday cake or sweets left over, prepare small packages for your friends, who will be happy to accept them as a post-party gift.

2. Give each small guest his or her party favor, so that they leave with a big smile and happy memories of the party.

Kitchen Parties!

Cakes etc....14 Let's bake cookies...30 For your special day, Mommy...38 Slumber party...48 Chocolate mania...62

Cakes etc...

(FOR BOYS 👦 AND GIRLS 👧 AGED 5 AND ABOVE)

Invite a group of children to the birthday party you want to have in the kitchen, with a confectionary theme. Make sure the group includes at least one or two older children who can help the younger ones or distribute roles to all the members of the group. Kids love playing in the kitchen and you will be pleasantly surprised by how responsible they can be if you show them you trust them.

Share out the ingredients the children will need into plastic bowls and give them the right measuring cups and spoons, so that they can truly learn how to work properly in the kitchen. If you have enough space, divide the kids into two groups and give each one a name, e.g. «the pink spoons» and «the blue spoons» or «chili peppers» and «fried green tomatoes» for girls and boys. Decide on the number of guests according to the space you have available. The older children can perform the more difficult tasks, such as reading the recipe, breaking or separating the eggs or operating the mixer. However, when it's time to bake the cake, you should help them put it in and take it out of the oven. Your help may also be required with the use of small electrical appliances.

Once the children have prepared the cake mix, let them choose the baking pan they will bake it in. Buy at least two or three different pans, shaped as a doll, a dog, a teddy bear, a princess castle, a computer, a rabbit or a car, and allow them to choose which one they like best. Give them paint brushes and oil to grease the inside of the pan. While the cake is baking, you can offer the kids glasses of milk and cookies or muffins prepared in advance for this original party. Don't forget that working in the kitchen gives everyone an appetite, and kids even more so.

After they have eaten, they can perform some less difficult tasks, such as preparing giant muffins that don't need beating in the mixer. You will need jumbo muffin pans, as well as jumbo paper muffin cups

Super chocolate Muffins

Yields 6 jumbo muffins
Preparation time 15 minutes
Baking time 15 minutes (200˚C/400˚F)
Suitable for freezing
Degree of difficulty ☺

- 2 cups cake flour, not self-raising
- 1 tablespoon baking powder
- 1/4 teaspoon bicarbonate of soda
- 1/4 teaspoon salt
- 1/2 cup (1 stick) unsalted butter, melted
- 50g (2oz) melted chocolate
- 1 large egg
- 1/4 cup unsweetened cocoa
- 2/3 cup brown sugar
- 1 teaspoon vanilla essence
- 2/3 cup (200g) yogurt
- 1 cup milk
- 1 cup chocolate chips

1. Sift together the flour, baking powder, soda and salt in a large bowl. Melt the butter with the chocolate. In another bowl, beat the egg lightly, add the melted chocolate butter, the cocoa, sugar, vanilla, yogurt and milk and mix gently with a fork.

2. Fold in the chocolate chips and pour the liquid mixture into the bowl with the dry ingredients. Mix briskly with a fork, enough for the solid liquids to moisten. Do not over-mix the ingredients. The mixture must be lumpy, not smooth.

3. Butter the holes of a jumbo muffin pan well, or line them with baking cups. Fill 2/3 of the molds with the mixture and bake the muffins at 200˚C (400˚F) for 20-25 minutes. For extra large muffins, fill the molds to the rim. Remove to a rack and let cool. If you like, stick an original chef cocktail stick into each muffin. Can be stored in the freezer, hermetically sealed in food bags.

Savory muffins with bacon

Yields 6 jumbo, 12 regular or 24 mini muffins
Preparation time 25 minutes
Baking time 20-25 minutes (200˚C/400˚F)
Suitable for freezing
Degree of difficulty ☺

- 1 cup cake flour, not self-raising
- 1 cup corn-starch
- 1 tablespoon baking powder
- 1/8 teaspoon bicarbonate of soda
- 1 teaspoon salt
- 1 teaspoon sugar
- 1 teaspoon paprika
- 2 large eggs
- 1 cup milk
- 1/3 cup melted butter (2/3 stick)
- 1/3 cup finely chopped red and green peppers
- 4 bacon rashers, finely chopped

1. Make sure that all the ingredients are at room temperature. Brush a 12-hole standard muffin pan or a 6-hole jumbo muffin pan with corn oil. If you wish, you can omit the oil and use paper baking cups.

2. Mix the first 7 ingredients in a large bowl. In another bowl, beat the eggs and milk lightly. Sauté the peppers in the butter, and once cold, mix with the rest of the liquid ingredients.

3. Pour the liquid mixture into the bowl with the flour and stir briskly with a fork, just enough to moisten the solids. Sauté the pieces of bacon until crispy. Drain on absorbent paper. Add to the rest of the ingredients and mix in.

4. Fill the muffin pan with the mixture, 2/3 of the way to the rim. If you like, sprinkle over a little grated hard cheese. Bake the savory muffins in the oven at 200˚C (400˚F) for 25 minutes. Remove from the oven, let stand in the pan for 10 minutes, overturn onto an oven rack and let cool. Can be stored in the freezer, in hermetically sealed food bags.

Choco-chip Vanilla muffins

Yields 6 jumbo, 12 regular or 24 mini muffins
Preparation time 15 minutes
Baking time 20-25 minutes (200˚C/400˚F)
Suitable for freezing
Degree of difficulty ☺

- 2 cups cake flour, not self-raising
- 1/2 cup caster sugar
- 1 tablespoon baking powder
- 1/8 teaspoon salt
- 1 cup chocolate chips
- 1 large egg
- 1/3 cup (2/3 stick) unsalted butter, melted
- 1 cup milk
- 2/3 cup (200g) yogurt
- 2 teaspoons vanilla essence

1. Mix the flour, sugar, baking powder and salt in a large bowl. Add and mix in the chocolate chips. In a small bowl, beat the egg lightly, then add the butter, milk, yogurt and vanilla, and beat with a fork until blended.

2. Add the liquid mixture to the flour and stir, just enough to moisten the solids. Do not mix the ingredients too much. The mixture must be lumpy, not smooth.

3. Butter the cases of a muffin pan well, or line them with baking cups. Fill the cups up to 2/3 with the mixture and bake the muffins at 200˚C (400˚F) for 20-25 minutes. Remove to a rack and let cool. Can be stored in the freezer, in hermetically sealed food bags.

Yields 12 cupcakes
Preparation time 30 minutes
Baking time 45 minutes (175°C/350°F)
Suitable for freezing
Degree of difficulty ☺

• 1 recipe perfect chocolate cake
  (recipe on page 23)
• two 6-hole teddy bear baking pans
• colored icing in tubes, for decorating
• 12 paper baking cups (regular size)

1. Prepare the perfect chocolate cake mixture and pour it into the 12 teddy bear molds, previously buttered and floured thoroughly. Bake the teddy bears for 40-45 minutes at 175°C (350°F). Remove from the oven and let cool enough to handle.
2. Using a sharp knife, make a horizontal slot near the middle of each teddy bear, without cutting through to the other side. Insert the little paper cup ballet skirts while the cakes are still warm, so that they stick when cold.
3. Transfer the cakes to a platter and garnish with colored icing. Will keep in the freezer for up to 6 months.

Chocolate fudge sauce

Yields 3 cups
Preparation time 15 minutes
Degree of difficulty ☺

- 2 tablespoons (1/4 stick) butter
- 100g (4oz) dark chocolate
- 1/2 cup sugar
- 1/3 cup unsweetened cocoa
- 1 cup (400g or 16oz) dark corn syrup
- 1/2 cup double cream
- 2 teaspoons vanilla essence

1. Put the butter and chocolate in a saucepan and heat over low heat, until the chocolate melts. Add all the remaining ingredients except for the cream and vanilla essence, increase the heat and let the mixture boil. Stir for 2 minutes over high heat.

2. Remove from the heat, and stir the cream and vanilla in vigorously. Serve the warm sauce poured over fluffy scoops of vanilla ice cream. Can also be used for a mouthwatering fruit and marshmallow fondue.

Chocolate filling with cream cheese

To cover or fill a 22-cm (9-in) cake
Preparation time 15 minutes + 20 minutes refrigeration
Degree of difficulty ☺

- 125g (4oz) dark chocolate
- 1 cup (2 sticks) unsalted butter
- 200g (8oz) cream cheese, softened
- 3-4 tablespoons milk
- 2 teaspoons vanilla essence
- 2½ cups icing sugar

1. Melt the chocolate in a double boiler, remove from the heat and let cool. Cream the butter in the mixer. Add the cream cheese, milk and vanilla essence and beat until the ingredients are all joined together. Pour in the melted chocolate and sugar and beat, to obtain a smooth and homogeneous mixture.

2. Place the icing in the refrigerator for 20 minutes to set. Remove from the fridge, beat again until soft and use as a filling for cakes or as icing.

3. If you like, you can add 100g (4oz) coarsely ground roasted almonds to the chocolate filling. **For gianduja flavor** mix the chocolate cream with 1/3 cup chocolate hazelnut spread and 100g (4oz) roasted hazelnuts, coarsely ground.

- 3½ cups self-raising flour
- 1 cup sugar
- 1 cup brown sugar
- 1/2 teaspoon bicarbonate of soda and 1/2 teaspoon salt
- 1 cup milk
- 1 cup (2 sticks) soft margarine
- 4 eggs
- 125g (4oz) dark chocolate, melted
- 1 teaspoon vanilla essence
- 1/2 teaspoon red food coloring (optional)

Devil's food cake

1. Place all the cake ingredients in the mixer bowl and beat for 1 minute at low speed. Beat for another 3 minutes at high speed.
2. Thoroughly butter a large round cake mold with a hole in the middle, and pour in the mixture. Bake the cake at 180°C (360°F) for 1 hour. Remove from the oven and let cool on an oven rack.
Cut the cake into three layers, if you like, and join them with chocolate cream cheese filling (recipe on page 21).

- 1 cup cake flour, not self-raising
- 1/2 cup icing sugar
- 10 egg whites from medium eggs
- 1½ teaspoons cream of tartar
- 1/4 teaspoon salt
- 3/4 cup sugar
- 1 teaspoon vanilla or bitter almond essence

Angel food cake

1. Sift the flour with the icing sugar. Beat the egg whites, cream of tartar and salt in the mixer at high speed, until frothy and stiff. Gradually beat in the sugar sprinkling 1/4 cup at a time, beating well after each addition, until the egg whites form a thick, white shiny meringue that will stand. Gently fold in the essence.
2. Fold the flour into the meringue a little at a time, mixing gently with a wooden spoon, taking care not to deflate the meringue. Fill a large, ungreased Angel food cake baking pan with the mixture, one spoonful at a time, taking care not to leave air pockets. Bake the cake at 190°C (375°F), for 35-40 minutes.
3. Remove from the oven and let the cake cool in the pan, upside down so that it does not deflate. When cool, remove from the pan. To remove the cake more easily, pass the blade of a knife between the cake and the sides of the pan, to separate the two, and overturn onto a platter. Tap the pan lightly with your palm, and the cake will drop onto the platter.
4. Alternatively, replace 1/4 cup flour with cocoa, for a chocolate angel food cake.

- 1 cup (2 sticks) soft margarine
- 2 cups sugar
- 2 eggs
- 1 teaspoon bitter almond extract
- 1 teaspoon vanilla essence
- 1½ teaspoons vinegar
- 1½ cups (400g) yogurt
- 1¾ cups cake flour, not self-raising
- 3/4 cup unsweetened cocoa (top quality)
- 1½ teaspoons bicarbonate of soda

Very rich, very dark, very chocolate cake

1. Beat the margarine and sugar until creamy. Add the eggs and the essences and beat into the mixture. Add the vinegar and yogurt and beat for 1 minute. Sift the flour with the cocoa and pour into the mixer bowl. Beat the ingredients at high speed for a further 2 minutes.
2. Pour the cake batter into a large cake pan or two small round baking pans if you want to make sponge bases for cakes. Bake the cake for 50 minutes at 180°C (360°F), and the sponge bases for 45 minutes at 175°C (350°F), or until a skewer comes out dry.

- 2 cups self-raising flour
- 2 cups sugar
- 1/4 teaspoon bicarbonate of soda
- 1 cup unsweetened cocoa
- 1/4 teaspoon salt
- 5 large eggs
- 1/2 cup milk
- 1 cup (2 sticks) unsalted butter or soft margarine
- 2 teaspoons vanilla essence
- 1/3 cup boiling water
- 100g (4oz) chocolate chips mixed with 2 tablespoons flour (optional)

Perfect Chocolate cake

1. Place all the cake ingredients in the mixer bowl, in the order shown in the list, except for the boiling water and chocolate chips. Beat for 3 minutes. Stop beating, pour in the boiling water and beat for 1 minute. Fold in the chocolate chips.
2. For hand mixers: First cream the sugar and the butter until fluffy. Add the milk a little at a time, then the vanilla and beat to a smooth mixture. Mix the flour and soda, cocoa and salt and pour them into the bowl, alternating with the eggs. Beat for 3 minutes. Pour in the hot water and beat it into the mixture.
3. Butter and flour a baking pan and pour in the dough. Bake the cake at 175°C (350°F) for 45-50 minutes, or until a skewer comes out dry. Overturn the cake onto a rack and let it cool. Dust with icing sugar or cover with easy chocolate icing or ganache (recipes on page 29).

* recipe on page 27

24

Hara's Strawberry Cake

Daphne's Doll Cake

Yields 1 recipe
(for 25-28 cm/ 9-10 in baking pans)
Preparation time 25 minutes
Baking time 50 minutes (180°C/360°F)
<u>Suitable for freezing</u>
Degree of difficulty ☺

- 5 egg whites
- 1 egg
- 3 cups self-raising flour
- 2 cups caster sugar
- 1 cup strawberry-flavored yogurt
- 2/3 cup olive oil
- 1/2 cup buttermilk
- 2 teaspoons vanilla essence
- 1 teaspoon strawberry essence
- a few drops of red food coloring

1. Place all the ingredients in the mixer bowl and beat for 4 minutes, to form a smooth, fluffy and homogeneous mixture. Transfer the mixture to a well-buttered and floured baking pan and bake the cake at 180°C (360°F) for 45-50 minutes.

- 1 recipe strawberry cake
- 1 doll-shaped cake mold
- colored icing in tubes

1. With the help of her friends, Daphne prepared the doll cake and decorated it herself, using all her favorite colors. Daphne, Nefeli and Hara measured the strawberry cake ingredients in the mixer bowl, beat them and poured them into a doll-shaped mold, which Marilena had previously greased. Mommy helped a little with the oven, and when the cake was baked, they couldn't wait for it to cool.
2. When the cake cooled down, Daphne did the decorating herself using colored icing. Her imagination was her only guide as she created the doll's hair and dress with all the beautiful colors.

Yields 16 portions
Preparation time 1 hour
Baking time 1 hour 10 minutes (180°C/360°F)
Degree of difficulty ☺☺☺

- 1½ recipes chocolate or vanilla cake
- 1 round baking pan, diameter 26 cm (10in), height 10 cm (4in)

For the Mexican chocolate filling
- 200 g (8oz) dark chocolate, melted
- 2 egg yolks
- 4-5 tablespoons milk
- a little cinnamon and clove powder
- 2½ cups icing sugar
- 2 tablespoons butter

For decorating
- 1/2 cup apricot jam, heated and sieved
- 500g (1lb) readymade marzipan
- 1 packet (500g/1lb) readymade Regalice (sugar paste)
- special cookery markers for drawing on Regalice (various colors)

1. ATTENTION: for this cake, use only special cookery markers with food coloring for cakes. The Regalice must be decorated before the cake is refrigerated or frozen as the humidity resulting from refrigeration may not allow the marking of the icing with the food color markers. Therefore, prepare the cake with the chocolate filling only if you intend to decorate it immediately after baking it. If you plan to store the cake for the kids to decorate the next day, prepare the cake, without the filling, cover it with the marzipan and Regalice and store it uncovered at room temperature, for the icing to dry. The cake does not dry up easily, as two layers of icing protect it.

2. Prepare the chocolate cake recipe and pour it into a large round 26-cm (10in) baking pan, well buttered and with non-stick paper spread on the bottom, also buttered. Bake the cake at 180°C (360°F) for 1 hour to 1 hour 10 minutes. When the cake has been in the oven for 1 hour, stick a long wooden skewer into the center. If it comes out clean, the cake is ready, if not, let it cook for another 10 minutes. Remove the cake from the oven, overturn it onto a platter spread with non-stick paper, and let it cool.

3. Prepare the filling. Melt the chocolate over low heat. Beat the egg yolks with the milk and mix them with the chocolate. Add the icing sugar and spices and mix well. Finally, blend in the butter. Divide the cake into 3 layers, and join them with the chocolate filling. To make the cake softer, you can sprinkle the layers with a little strawberry syrup. Place the cake in the refrigerator until the filling sets.

4. For better results and a smoother surface, initially cover the cake with a thin layer of marzipan. You will find recipes for homemade marzipan and sugar paste on pages 209 and 113 respectively. Knead the marzipan on a surface sprinkled with icing sugar until soft. Roll it out into a thin sheet using a rolling pin, also sprinkled with icing sugar. Gently roll the sheet around the rolling pin and transfer it over the cake surface. Unroll carefully, so as to spread the marzipan over the cake and cover the top and sides. Pat down with your hands to smooth its surface.

5. Knead the Regalice lightly on a surface sprinkled with icing sugar, until soft. Roll out a smooth thin sheet of the paste with a rolling pin sprinkled with icing sugar. Make the sheet large enough to cover the top and sides of the cake. Wrap the Regalice around a cooking rod and transfer it over the cake. Unfold carefully and spread it over the cake. When the icing is dry, after 1 hour at room temperature, draw on it carefully using special markers with food coloring, which are non-toxic and suitable for writing on iced cakes. Store the cake uncovered in the freezer or refrigerator, until serving time.

Cookie dough to keep in the fridge

Yields 24 cookies
Preparation time 20 minutes
Baking time 10 minutes (200°C/400°F)
Degree of difficulty ☺

- 1 cup (2 sticks) unsalted butter
- 1 cup caster sugar
- 2 eggs
- 2 teaspoons vanilla essence
- 2 cups plain flour
- 1/4 teaspoon bicarbonate of soda
- a little salt
- 40g (1oz) dark chocolate, melted

1. Beat the butter with the sugar until white and fluffy. Add the eggs one at a time, and continue beating after each addition. Pour and mix in the vanilla essence.

2. Sift all the solid ingredients together and pour them into the bowl with the creamed butter. Knead the mixture with your hands to make soft and pliable dough. Divide the dough into two sections and knead one half with the melted chocolate.

3. Knead the white and chocolate dough to make two rolls, cover them with plastic wrap and refrigerate until firm. Cut 3-mm (0.1in) thick slices from each roll and cut out heart or animal cookies from the center of each slice with pastry cutters.

4. Place the chocolate shapes inside the white slices, and vice versa, and arrange the cookies on an unbuttered cookie sheet. Bake them for 8-10 minutes in a preheated oven at 200°C (400°F). Remove from the oven, let cool and place the cookies in small bags to give to the young chefs as they leave. The dough will keep for 2-3 days in the refrigerator, covered.

Butter cookies

Yields 40 small and large cookies
Preparation time 30 minutes
Baking time 15-20 minutes (180°C/360°F)
Degree of difficulty ☺

- 1 cup (2 sticks) unsalted butter
- 1 cup sugar
- 1 large egg
- 1 teaspoon vanilla essence
- 3 cups cake flour, not self-raising
- 1 teaspoon baking powder

1. Cream together the butter and sugar until white and fluffy, about 10 minutes. Stir in the egg and vanilla. Sift the flour and baking powder into a large bowl. Continue beating the liquid ingredients, and add the flour a little at a time. The dough will be very thick, so mix in the last part of flour with your hands. For chocolate cookies, add 125 g (4oz) melted baking chocolate to the dough and knead to incorporate.
2. Roll out the dough and cut different-shaped cookies with assorted pastry cutters. Arrange them on an ungreased baking tray. Bake the cookies for 10-20 minutes, depending on size, in a preheated oven at 200°C (400°F). If you bake more than one tray of cookies at a time, bake them in a fan-heated oven at 180°C (360°F).

Chocolate cookies

Yields 24 cookies
Preparation time 1 hour
Baking time 20 minutes (180°C/360°F)
Degree of difficulty ☺☺

- 1 cup (2 sticks) unsalted butter
- 1¼ cups icing sugar
- 1 teaspoon vanilla essence
- 1/2 cup unsweetened cocoa
- 1/8 teaspoons salt
- 1¾ cups cake flour, not self-raising
- 400g (14oz) dark baking chocolate
- 1 teaspoon vegetable oil

1. Beat the butter with the icing sugar and vanilla, until white and fluffy. Add the cocoa with the salt, and beat in to the mixture. Use the mixer's dough hook and add the flour gradually. Continue beating to form soft and elastic dough.
2. Roll out a sheet of the dough with a rolling pin, and cut out hearts, stars and teddy bears, about 4 mm thick and 5-7 cm wide. Arrange them on an unbuttered baking tray and bake them in a preheated oven at 185°C (370°F) for 15 to 20 minutes.
3. Remove from the oven and let cool on a grid. In the meantime, melt the chocolate with the oil in a small deep saucepan. Let it cool slightly and then dip half of each cookie into the chocolate. Place the chocolate-coated cookies on greaseproof paper and let them stand for several hours, until the chocolate sets.

Basic gingerbread dough

Yealds 40 biscuits or 2 gingerbread houses
Preparation time 30 minutes
Refrigeration time 1 hour
Baking time 15-25 minutes (180°C/360°F)
Degree of difficulty ☺

- 4½-5½ cups all-purpose flour
- 1 teaspoon bicarbonate of soda
- 1/2 teaspoon baking powder
- 1½ teaspoons salt
- 2-4 teaspoons ginger powder
- 1 teaspoon ground allspice
- 1 teaspoon ground cinnamon
- 1 teaspoon clove powder
- 1 cup vegetable shortening
- 1 cup brown sugar
- 2 eggs
- 1 cup dark corn syrup or molasses or maple syrup

1. Sift the flour, baking soda, baking powder, salt and spices together. Beat the butter and sugar in the mixer until fluffy. Add the eggs and syrup or molasses and continue beating, until well blended. The cookies will be lighter colored if you use dark corn syrup or maple syrup.
2. Continue beating in the mixer with the dough hook at low speed. Gradually add the solid ingredients mixture. The dough must be soft but not sticky. If it is sticky, add another 2-3 spoonfuls of flour. Divide the dough into 4 parts, cover them with plastic wrap and let stand in the refrigerator for 1 hour.
3. Cut pieces of the dough and roll them out with a small rolling pin on a floured surface or directly onto a slightly floured ungreased baking tray. If you want, line the baking sheets with ungreased parchment paper. Roll out the dough into a thin sheet. Cut shapes out of the dough with various pastry cutters. If your cookies are going to become Christmas tree decorations, pierce a large hole in them using a wooden skewer or a miniature round pastry cutter, so you can thread the ribbon through when they are baked.
4. Bake the cookies in the center of the oven for 15-20 minutes depending on size, in a preheated oven at 180°C (360°F). If you want to bake more than one tray at a time, use a fan-heated oven.

Two-toned cookies

Yields 20 cookies (different sizes)
Preparation time 1 hour
Baking time 10-15 minutes (175°C/350°F)
Degree of difficulty ☺☺

- 1 recipe spritz biscuit dough
  (recipe on page 37)
- red, green, blue, yellow food coloring

1. Divide the dough into two parts and leave one its natural color. Divide the second part into 2 or 3 bowls, depending on the number of colors you want to use, and color one section pink with a few drops of red food coloring, and the other blue or green. Place the dough into piping bags or cookie bags with 1-cm (0.4in) nozzles and pipe alternate rows of colored and white dough onto non-stick paper in a baking tray, leaving a small distance between rows.

2. Cover the rows with a large piece of non-stick paper and pass the rolling pin over it, to join the rows and form a 3-mm (0.1in/ paper thin) thick sheet. At this stage, refrigerate the dough for 15 minutes, or until the dough is firm enough to cut.

3. Cut out two-toned striped cookies in any shape you want, hearts, butterflies, flowers, stars or Christmas trees, using various pastry cutters. Remove the cookies with a cookie spatula and place them one next to the other on an unbuttered baking tray. Join the leftover pieces of dough, knead them lightly and cut out more two-tone cookies.

4. Bake the cookies on the bottom shelf of the oven at 175°C (350°F) for 10-15 minutes, depending on the size, or until the edges start to become golden brown. Remove from the oven and transfer to a rack to cool, using a cookie spatula.

Spritz biscuits

Yields 72 biscuits
Preparation time 30 minutes
Baking time 10 minutes (180°C/360°F)
Degree of difficulty ☺

- 4 cups plain flour
- 1 teaspoon baking powder
- a little salt
- 1½ cups (3 sticks) soft unsalted butter or white vegetable shortening
- 1 cup sugar
- 1 teaspoon vanilla essence
- 1 egg
- 4 tablespoons milk
- food coloring

1. Mix the flour, baking powder and salt in a bowl. Beat the butter, sugar and vanilla in the mixer at medium speed, until creamy. Add the egg and milk and beat to a smooth mixture.

2. Continue beating and pour the solid ingredients into the mixer bowl, one spoonful at a time, to form soft dough. Don't use all the solid ingredients if the dough becomes too thick. Do not refrigerate the mixture.

3. To make spritz biscuits, you will need a spritz cookie press. Choose a metal one for better results. Attach the disc you want to use to the press. Fill the spritzer with 1/4 of the dough and pipe out daisy-shaped biscuits by pressing the metal handle down onto an unbuttered baking tray. Divide the rest of the dough into bowls and color it with different shades of food coloring. Attach different discs to the spritzer to make heart-shaped spritz biscuits with pink dough, garlands or trees with green dough or stars with yellow dough.

4. Bake the biscuits in a pre-heated oven at 180°C (360°F) for 8-10 minutes. Remove from the oven and let cool on a cookie rack. If you like, brush the biscuits with a little egg white, and sprinkle them with crystal sugar.

For your special day, Mommy...

(FOR BOYS ☝ AND GIRLS ☺ AGED 8 AND ABOVE)

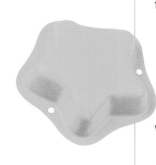

Mother's Day is always a great opportunity for children to make their mommies happy. So, kids, get organized to bake mommy a cake and prepare a special surprise for her special day.

For absolute secrecy, confide in daddy or grandma with your plans. But because secrecy is not a simple thing, especially if you plan to use an area used by the family every day, don't worry if mommy guesses your intentions. The greatest surprise will be the lovely cake you make for her and the fact that you will be using the kitchen creatively and giving her a rest for her special day.

Mother's Day is always on a Sunday, so get organized on the Saturday before and invite your friends to help you. Help is always welcome and working in the kitchen is more fun when you have company. Invite your friends and their mothers, and while you prepare the cakes, they can have coffee or tea in the kitchen, served by you.

One great surprise is to show mommy that you can be a serious confectioner and clean up after yourself. To make things easier, don't let all the utensils and bowls collect in the sink at the end of the day, when you will all be tired; make sure you clean each utensil right after you use it.

Don't hesitate to ask for mommy's help, which you will definitely need, in order to find out where she keeps all those useful objects that make baking 'a piece of cake'. First of all, you will need a measuring cup and measuring spoons for all the ingredients you must use. You will also need a large mixer bowl and the mixer, for beating all the ingredients of the cake you choose to make. Spatulas, plastic or metal bowls for the ingredients and baking pans are absolute necessities. The right baking pan will make your cake a perfect success. Finally, you will need mommy's help with the oven. Never try to operate the oven if mommy or daddy is not around!

Men are traditionally the best chefs, so there is no reason to exclude boys from this party. Girls, prepare yourselves, the men in the group will surprise you with their baking abilities!

Read the recipe carefully, note the ingredients you will need and check your supplies. Obtain everything you need, so that you are not missing things when you start cooking.

RECIPES FOR KIDS

(supervised by an adult)

✧ Pink Lemonade

✧ Pink lemonade Chiffon cake

✧ Petits fours

✧ Mocha and cream cake

✧ Spicy apple muffins

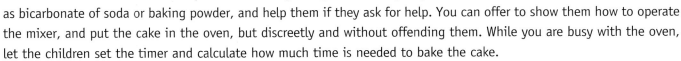

Instructions for mothers:

Mother's Day is always on a Sunday, so you can organize a pleasant Saturday morning by inviting your child's friends over to work and have fun in the kitchen baking cakes and making other sweets. Don't think that children are incapable of making even the most intricate cake. Answer their questions relating to ingredients they might not know, such as bicarbonate of soda or baking powder, and help them if they ask for help. You can offer to show them how to operate the mixer, and put the cake in the oven, but discreetly and without offending them. While you are busy with the oven, let the children set the timer and calculate how much time is needed to bake the cake.

For a girls only party, a good idea is to let them dress up in adult clothes, high heels, boas, hats and jackets from their mothers' wardrobes. The invitation might say "Come along dressed as your mom". Creating things in the kitchen is more fun if the kids see it as a game. As cooking always builds up an appetite, make sure you have some sweet bread and chocolate spread to serve to the little chefs, and drinks such as milk, strawberry or chocolate milkshakes and fruit juice.

Finally, urge the kids nicely to clean up after themselves and leave the kitchen tidy. You will be surprised by how much initiative they will take, if you trust them and treat them as adults. Your role will only be to inform and finish things off, without correcting their actions at every step. Say you have other work to do in the house and give them the independence to be creative. Have fun everyone, big and small!

PARENTS BEWARE: For a children's party in the kitchen, read and follow the instructions on page 15 carefully.

RECIPES WITH MOMMY'S HELP

✧ Lady apples

✧ Almond and chocolate chip chiffon cake

✧ Light orange cheesecake

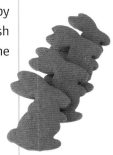

Chiffon cake with almonds and chocolate chips

Yields 14 pieces
Preparation time 40 minutes
Baking time 1 hour (160°C/325°F)
Degree of difficulty ☺☺☺

For the cake
- 200g (8oz) chocolate chips, ground in the blender
- 2¼ cups cake flour, not self-raising
- 1½ cups caster sugar
- 1 teaspoon baking powder
- 1/2 cup olive oil
- 6 extra large eggs, separated
- 1/2 cup water
- 1 teaspoon vanilla essence
- 1 teaspoon bitter almond essence
- 1/4 teaspoon cream of tartar
- 1½ cups blanched and roasted almond slices
- 1 angel food cake pan

For the icing
- 1½ cups icing sugar
- 2-3 tablespoons milk
- 1/2 teaspoon bitter almond essence
- 1 egg white, beaten to a soft meringue

1. Preheat the oven to 180°C (360°F). Mix the flour, 1 cup sugar, baking powder and a pinch of salt in a large bowl. Make a hole in the center and pour in the oil, egg yolks, water and food coloring.

2. Beat the ingredients in the mixer at medium speed for 4 minutes, until the mixture thickens. Mix the ground chocolate chips with 2 tablespoons flour, and add them to the mixer bowl.

3. Place the egg whites and cream of tartar in a clean mixer bowl and beat them with clean dry whisks until frothy. Continue beating and add the sugar, a little at a time, to make a thick meringue that will stand. Fold spoonfuls of the meringue into the mixture with the other ingredients, to make it thinner. Then incorporate the rest of the meringue into the mixture, with gentle strokes, taking care not to deflate it. Pour the cake mix into an unbuttered angel food cake mold. Make sure you don't leave any air pockets as you pour the mixture into the mold.

4. Place the cake on the lower oven shelf and bake it for 1 hour. Remove from the oven and overturn the mold onto a rack. Let it cool in the mold for 1 hour 30 minutes.

5. Separate the cake from the mold sides with a knife, and transfer it to a serving platter. Mix all the icing ingredients together and pour half the icing over the cake. Sprinkle the surface with the almonds and cover with the rest of the icing. Sprinkle with shiny blue sugar. Will keep for 4 days in the refrigerator.

Yields 18 apple muffins
Preparation time 20 minutes
Baking time 25 minutes (200°C/400°F)
Degree of difficulty ☺

- 2 large apples in cubes, steamed
- 1 cup coarsely ground hazelnuts
- 1 cup finely chopped sultanas
- 2/3 cup plain flour
- 2/3 cup sugar
- 1/3 cup fine semolina
- 4 eggs
- 1 cup soft margarine
- 1/4 cup Cognac
- 1 teaspoon ground cinnamon
- 2 teaspoons baking powder
- icing sugar and cinnamon or colored icing in a tube

Spicy Apple Muffins

1. Purée the apple cubes using a fork. Place the purée into a bowl and add the remaining ingredients. Mix them all together briskly with a spoon, to form a smooth soft mixture.

2. Place colored paper cases in the holes of two muffin trays, holding 12 and 6 muffins respectively. Pour the mixture into the cases, covering 2/3 of the height. Bake the muffins for 20-25 minutes at 200°C (400°F), until they rise. Remove from the oven and let cool on a rack. Before serving, sprinkle with icing sugar and cinnamon, or write a message using colored icing in a tube.

Lady Apples

Yields 8 apples
Preparation time 30 minutes
Degree of difficulty ☺☺

- 8 small red firm apples
- 8 small lollipop sticks
- 1/2 cup water
- 2 cups sugar
- 1/2 cup corn syrup (glucose)
- a few drops red food coloring
- 1 cup coarsely ground hazelnuts
  or almonds

Attention: adult super-vision is necessary for this recipe, as it includes hot caramel.

1. Wash the apples thoroughly, and dry them. Remove the stalks and insert the lollipop sticks. Line a flat tray that will fit on the oven shelf with waxed paper.

2. Place the water, sugar and corn syrup in a clean and dry non-stick pan. Mix with a wooden spoon over high heat, just to combine. Stop stirring and let the syrup boil. As soon as it comes to the boil, add the coloring. Do not stir the syrup at all. Count exactly 12 minutes, and your caramel will be ready. If you have a caramel thermometer, dip it inside the caramel but make sure it doesn't touch the bottom of the pan, and let it reach 120°C (245°F). One experiment that will show you if the caramel is ready is to dip a clean dry spoon in it. Take a little caramel and pour it immediately into a glass of water. If it forms a hard ball, then your caramel is ready.

3. Remove the pan from the heat and dip it into a larger pan with warm water, to stop the boiling. Hold the apples by the lollipop sticks and dip them into the hot caramel one by one. Twist them so that the entire surface is covered. As you remove them from the caramel, dip the base in the ground hazelnuts and then stand them on non-stick paper. Refrigerate for 15 minutes, for the caramel to set, and the lady apples are ready to serve. Will keep for 1 day, at room temperature.

Mocha cake with cream filling

Yields 14 pieces or 24 muffins
Preparation time 20 minutes
Baking time 1 hour (180°C/360°F)
Degree of difficulty ☺☺

- 200g (8oz) cream cheese, softened
- 2 tablespoons icing sugar
- 2 tablespoons Kahlua or cocoa liqueur
- 3 cups self-raising flour
- 1/4 teaspoon salt
- 1²/₃ cups sugar
- 2/3 cup (1½ sticks) margarine
- 4 eggs
- 3 tablespoons instant coffee and
  1/2 teaspoon vanilla powder
- 3 tablespoons cocoa powder
- 2/3 cup single cream

1. Combine the cream cheese with the sugar and liqueur in a small bowl.

2. Put the rest of the ingredients in the mixer bowl and beat for 4 minutes at medium speed, until soft.

3. Preheat the oven to 180°C (360°F). Butter and flour a ring cake tin thoroughly. Pour the cake mixture into the pan, and make a small opening in the middle of the mixture, all the way round, using the back of a spoon. Spoon the cream cheese mixture into the opening carefully.

4. Alternatively, line two 12-muffin trays with paper baking cups. Fill each case with cake mix and top with 1/2 spoonful of filling.

5. Bake the cake at 180°C (360°F) for 50 minutes to 1 hour, or until a skewer comes out clean. If you make muffins, bake them for 25-30 minutes. As soon as you take the cake out of the oven, overturn it onto a platter to cool. Serve sprinkled with icing sugar mixed with a little vanilla powder.

Petit fours

Yields 24 petits fours
Preparation time 40 minutes
Baking time 15 minutes (180˚C/360˚F)
Degree of difficulty ☺☺☺

For the sponge cake
- 2 eggs
- 1/2 cup caster sugar
- 2/3 cup self-raising flour
- 2 tablespoons unsalted butter, melted

For the icing
- 1 cup apricot jam, heated
- 2 teaspoons apricot or
  orange-flavored liqueur (optional)
- 200g (8oz) readymade marzipan
- 1 jar (1lb – 450g)
  readymade icing
- 25 miniature sugar shapes to decorate

1. Preheat the oven to 180˚C (360˚F). Butter a square 20-cm (8-in) pan well, and line it with parchment paper, also buttered.

2. Beat the eggs and sugar in the mixer for 10 minutes, until the mixture rises and sets. Add all the flour at once and fold in the egg mixture very softly with a spoon. Add the melted butter and fold in again, very softly. Pour the mixture into the cake pan, and smooth it down with a spatula.

3. Place the cake in the center of the oven and bake it for 15 minutes. Remove from the oven and overturn onto a cloth sprinkled with icing sugar. Remove the paper carefully and let the sponge cake cool.

4. Using a square pastry cutter (4 cm/ 1.5 in), cut small squares out of the sponge cake. Mix the warm jam with the liqueur and use a brush to coat the sponge squares with this mixture. Roll out the marzipan with a small rolling pin into a thin sheet, on a surface sprinkled with icing sugar. Using the same pastry cutter as before cut 5 squares out of the marzipan and stick them onto each side of the sponge squares.

5. Heat the icing for 1 minute in the microwave or a saucepan at low heat, until soft. Place the petit fours on a rack and pour over the liquid icing. While the icing is soft, stick small sugared shapes onto the top of each petit four. When the icing is dry, store them covered at room temperature.

Light Orange Cheesecake

Yields 4 small cheesecakes (16 portions)
Preparation time 20 minutes
Baking time 1 hour 15 minutes (150°C/300°F)
Refrigeration time 3 hours
Degree of difficulty ☺☺☺

For the crumbly crust
- 1½ cups light digestive biscuits, ground
- 2 tablespoons shiny orange-colored crystal sugar
- 2 tablespoons orange zest
- 1/3 cup (2/3 stick) unsalted butter, melted

For the filling
- 3 200g (8oz) packets ricotta or light cream cheese
- 1/3 cup icing sugar
- 1 teaspoon vanilla essence
- 1 tablespoon orange zest
- 3 large eggs
- 3 tablespoons all-purpose flour
- 1/4 cup single cream or yogurt
- 2 tablespoons orange juice

1. Mix all the ingredients for the crust together and spread the mixture on the bottom of 4 very well-buttered cheesecake spring form molds (diameter: 10 cm/ 4 in). Cover the bottom and the sides and press down well with your fingers. Place the molds in the fridge while you prepare the filling.
2. Cream the ricotta with the sugar and vanilla at medium speed in the mixer, until the mixture is smooth, without lumps. While beating, add the eggs one by one, adding 1 tablespoon of flour after each egg. Mix the cream or yogurt with the orange juice, and pour into the mixer bowl. Turn the mixer to low speed and continue beating for a short while, long enough to mix in the cream.
3. Divide the mixture into the molds. Bake the cheesecakes at 230°C (450°F) for 15 minutes. Lower the oven to 150°C (300°F) and continue baking for 1 more hour. Switch off the oven and let the cheesecakes stand inside with the door half-open, until cool.
4. Put the cheesecakes in the refrigerator in their molds and let them stand for at least 3 hours, or overnight. Remove the molds and transfer to plates. Serve with pieces of glacé orange and rosettes of fluffy orange icing. Follow the recipe on page 69 for "pink icing" – omit the food coloring and add a little orange zest.

Pink lemonade

Yields 4-6 glasses lemonade
Preparation time 30 minutes
Degree of difficulty ☺

- 3 cups fresh raspberries or strawberries
- 1 cup caster sugar
- 3 cups water
- 3 cups lemon juice
- crushed ice, for serving

1. Boil the raspberries or strawberries with the sugar and water in a saucepan, until the mixture reduces to half the original volume. Pass the mixture through a fine sieve, leaving only the transparent liquid.
2. Pour into a large pitcher, add the juice, and stir. Serve with crushed ice.

Yields 14 pieces
Preparation time 25 minutes
Baking time 1 hour (160°C/325°F)
Degree of difficulty ☺☺

- 2½ cups self-raising flour
- 1/4 teaspoon salt
- 1½ cups caster sugar
- 4 large eggs, separated, and
  4 egg whites
- 1/2 cup corn oil
- 1/2 cup water
- 3 tablespoons lemon juice
- 2 tablespoons lemon zest
- 1 teaspoon lemon essence (optional)
- 1 teaspoon strawberry essence
- a few drops red food coloring
- 1/2 teaspoon cream of tartar
- 1 angel food cake mold

For decorating
- thin candy buttons
- 1 recipe easy lemon icing
  (recipe on page 29)
- halved sugared lemon slices

1. Preheat the oven to 160°C (325°F). Mix the flour, salt and 1 cup of the sugar in a bowl. Place the egg yolks, corn oil, water, juice, lemon zest and essence, strawberry essence and a few drops of red food coloring in the mixer bowl; beat them very, very lightly, just enough to join together. Add the solid ingredients and beat, to form a thick, smooth mixture.
2. Beat the 8 egg whites with the cream of tartar in a clean mixer bowl with clean whisks, until white. Add the remaining sugar and beat to form a meringue that holds stiff peaks. Initially fold 2-3 tablespoons of the meringue into the pink mixture, to dilute it. Pour the mixture into the bowl with the beaten egg whites and fold gently until combined, to make a light pink mixture.
3. Pour the cake batter into an ungreased angel food cake mold. Bake the cake for 1 hour on the oven's bottom shelf. Remove from the oven and overturn on a platter, together with the mold, and let cool. Pass a knife blade around the edges of the cake, to separate it from the mold, and transfer to a platter. Garnish with easy lemon icing, candy bottons and sugared lemon slices. The cake will keep for 4 days in the refrigerator.

Slumber Party...

(FOR BOYS AND GIRLS AGED 6 AND ABOVE)

Organize an unusual party by inviting your child's young friends to spend the night at your house. For an overnight party where you will be the only adult responsible for all the children attending, you must make sure the number of children attending is no more than you can handle. Four to six children is an ideal number, especially if the guests are still quite young. Also make sure that the children in the group are of the same gender, i.e. only girls or only boys, because this will help avoid fights, and the kids will have more interests in common. One older child, a brother or sister, or another member of the family will balance out the rest of the kids, taking on the role of leader. Remember that children take on roles in a group according to their character; the quieter ones need to be urged to participate, while one or two always stand out for their leadership qualities. It is preferable to have only one leader in a group of children, someone with the sense to quietly direct the game. Choose the children you invite carefully, because a disruptive child with leadership qualities may disrupt the entire party.

Make invitations out of white cardboard cut in the shape of a pillow. Stick on a few colored feathers or some cotton wool and write the party message inside. Mention that each guest is invited to attend the party with his/her "formal" pajama, and is free to bring along a bedtime friend. Many children sleep with a stuffed animal or doll, so remind them to bring it along, in order to avoid unforeseen reactions. Many children love the idea of sleeping at someone else's house, but are often frightened when the time comes.

Include the children in all the party preparations. As soon as they arrive at the house, they can put on their pajamas straight away, in order to feel comfortable and enjoy this party's special feeling. Gather them in the kitchen and urge them to participate in a creative

cooking game. Make one or two pizzas for the kids to fill according to their imagination. Share out the ingredients in small colored bowls and place them on the table. Give them butter and paintbrushes to use for coating the baking trays. Don't forget to explain what they are doing and why at each step. The trays are buttered so that the dough doesn't stick to them while baking. The more you tell the children, the more they will absorb. It is so simple to get close to them; all you have to do is talk, trust them and have faith that they will understand you.

When the pizzas are ready and while you bake them, get them to make the beds in the room where they are going to sleep. Share out pillows, sheets, blankets and duvets. Don't worry about the confusion; let them prepare their sleeping space by themselves. The kids will have most fun if they can eat their pizza on the beds while you tell them a good scary story, with plenty of humor, or a fairy tale they all know and like. Say goodnight and urge them to go to sleep. Of course, you can be sure that this won't happen, but that is the point of a slumber party: to have fun!

Next morning, gather all your young guests in the kitchen again, and let them help you prepare pancakes with honey and teddy bear fried eggs, and serve them milk and fruit juice. Parents should arrive to pick up their children quite early in the morning, as it is sure that they will all be lacking sleep.

RECIPES FOR THE NIGHT OF THE PARTY

✫ Strawberry Pizza

✫ Teddy Bear Pizza

✫ Vegetable Pizza

✫ Cream-filled vanilla cookies

✫ Blue dream cake

✫ Fantasy pinwheel cookies

RECIPES FOR THE MORNING AFTER

✫ Teddy bear sandwiches

✫ Teddy bear pancakes with honey

✫ Teddy bear fried eggs

✫ Hash browns

✫ Chocolate Thick-shakes

✫ Real Vanilla milkshakes

✫ Old-fashioned Banana milkshakes

Party diary

Katerina and Sonya's party

Two weeks before the party

1. Invite your child's young friends to this original party. As there are relatively few parties organized at this time of year in comparison to Spring or Christmas, you can give out the invitations 1 week before the party. It's a good idea to talk to all the parents on the telephone and explain how you intend to amuse the children. The invitation can be shaped like a pillow and made of cardboard, with cotton wool or thick white velvet or toweling material on the outside. It can also be decorated with small silver stars. Write the message on the inside.

2. You can prepare the pizza dough well in advance and spread it on well-buttered baking trays or perforated pizza pans. Cover with cling film and store the uncooked dough in the freezer until the night of the party. Defrost the dough for 1 hour before using. The dough will expand quite a lot in the freezer.

3. Prepare the cookies and cake. Store the former in a cookie tin and place the decorated cake in the freezer. After it has frozen well, take it out and wrap it securely with cling film. Store in the freezer for up to one month. The cake will keep for 2 days in the refrigerator.

4. Prepare the dough for the teddy bear bread and spread it on well-buttered trays. One tray will give you six buns. Make sure you have a second tray for more bread, if needed. Cover the dough without baking it, and place the trays in the freezer. The dough will rise and will be ready to bake when defrosted. Alternatively, you can bake the buns and store them in plastic bags in the freezer, once cool.

One week in advance

1. Read the recipes carefully and buy all the ingredients except for the vegetables. Prepare the cookies you want and store them in cookie tins. If you like, store a few in pretty bags or boxes to hand out to the kids at the end of the party.

On the day of the party

1. Buy the fresh vegetables. Prepare the ingredients that the children will need to make the pizzas, divide them into bowls, cover them with cling film and store them in the refrigerator.

2. Take the cake out of the freezer at least 7 hours before the party.

On the night of the party

1. Prepare the pizzas together with the children, so as to spend some creative time in the kitchen. When the kids have had their pizza, you can cut the cake.

Party games

1. A nice party gift could be a fabric doll made by the kids themselves during the party. Buy fabric in different colors, thick plaits of wool for the doll's hair, Styrofoam for stuffing, buttons for the eyes and nose, scissors and thick needles and special thread for children. This creative game will keep the children busy for several hours, as long as you keep them company and guide them through the process.

2. Another creative game is to encourage the children to make up short stories and write them in books that they will make themselves. Fold 10 A4 pages in half and perforate them at the folded end. Then fold a sheet of colored cardboard in half also, and perforate it in the same way. Thread some thin ribbon through the holes and tie it, making a book with cardboard covers. Give the children felt-tip pens, cookie cutters to make shapes with and one subject each, around which to create their own story.

The morning after

1. Prepare and cook the potatoes before the kids wake up, and keep them warm in the oven. Prepare the chocolate milkshakes. Cook the pancakes and eggs when the children are awake, so they can help. Encourage them to set a nice breakfast table, gather them all around it, and enjoy your breakfast with them.

Good Things for kids

Vegetable pizza: Homemade pizza is both tasty and healthy. By preparing it at home, you have control over the quality and freshness of the ingredients you use, and can therefore be sure of what your children are eating. If you like, you can add pieces of various vegetables (carrots, broccoli, red pepper, zucchini or other) to the tomato sauce, boil until soft and then purée it in the blender to obtain a thick smooth sauce that is both tasty and healthy.
Honey pancakes, fried eggs, fruit and milk smoothies: homemade tastes with healthy ingredients that will be appreciated by both the young guests and their mothers.
Homemade sandwich bread: Make your own sandwich bread and pizza dough, and avoid unnecessary preservatives.

Easy Vanilla Sponge Cake

Yields 1 recipe
Preparation time 25 minutes
Baking time 25 minutes
Suitable for freezing
Degree of difficulty ☺

1 small recipe
• 4 eggs
• 1 cup sugar
• 1 teaspoon vanilla extract
• 1 cup self-raising flour

1 large recipe
• 6 eggs
• 1½ cups sugar
• 1 teaspoon vanilla extract
• 1½ cups self-raising flour

1. For a round sponge cake, use a round 26-cm baking tin. For square sponge cakes, you will need a 24x24cm (10x10in) pan and for rolls, use a jellyroll pan. Line the pan you intend to use with greaseproof paper and butter well. You can also bake the sponge cake in a well-buttered anodized aluminum pan shaped like a doll, teddy bear, castle or car. For 30-cm (12-in) pans, use the large recipe.
2. Place the eggs and sugar in the mixer bowl. Beat them at high speed for 15-20 minutes, until they set and double in volume. Stir in the vanilla. Gradually sift the flour over the eggs, still beating at very low speed until it is incorporated into the mixture, taking great care not to deflate the eggs.
3. Pour the batter into the prepared pan and bake at 180°C (360°F) for 25-30 minutes, until the surface is golden brown or a skewer comes out clean. Overturn onto a towel sprinkled with icing sugar. Let the cake cool and slice it into layers, if you want. Store the sponge cake layers in an airtight container in the freezer for up to 6 months.

Marshmallows

Yields 20 large or 100 small marshmallows
Preparation time 30 minutes
Refrigeration time 12 hours
Degree of difficulty ☺☺☺

• 2 sachets (2 tablespoons) gelatine
• 1/2 cup cold water
• 2 cups caster sugar
• 3/4 cup light corn syrup (glucose)
• 3/4 cup water
• a few drops food coloring
• 2 teaspoons vanilla essence
• 1/4 cup icing sugar mixed with 1/4 cup cornstarch

1. Dissolve the gelatine in 1/2 cup cold water in the mixer bowl. Let it rise for 10 minutes. Coat the sides of the mixer bowl with a little oil. Also coat a medium non-stick saucepan with oil. Add the sugar, glucose and 3/4 cup water. Mix over medium heat until the sugar melts. Stop stirring and let the syrup boil.
2. As soon as it comes to the boil, add the food coloring, if used. Dip the caramel thermometer into the syrup. As soon as it reaches 120°C (245°F), remove it from the heat. If you don't have a thermometer, count exactly 12 minutes. Also, after about 10 minutes, test the syrup by taking a little of the mixture out of the pan with a clean dry spoon and dropping it into a glass of water. If it forms a hard ball straight away, the syrup is ready.
3. Pour the syrup with a slow steady flow into the gelatine mixture, beating at medium speed. The whole process should take about 15 minutes. Add the vanilla to the mixture after all the syrup has been incorporated. At this stage, the marshmallow mixture will be very soft and light.
4. Coat or spray a jellyroll pan with corn oil. Sprinkle over a little icing sugar and cornstarch mixture. Pour in the marshmallow mixture and sprinkle with half of the remaining sugar-cornstarch mixture. Refrigerate overnight, until set.
5. Remove the pan from the refrigerator and overturn onto your work surface, which should be sprinkled with icing sugar and cornstarch. Dip pastry cutters into hot water and cut out any shapes you like. Roll them in the sugar and cornstarch again. Stand on a rack for 1 hour to dry. Store in airtight containers. Will keep fresh for up to 10 days.

For fruity marshmallows: Substitute the water with orange, cherry or other fruit juice, except pineapple, when you dissolve the gelatine. If you use water, you can still make fruity marshmallows by adding your favorite Jell-O instead of plain gelatine.

For peppermint-flavored marshmallows: Instead of vanilla, add 1 teaspoon peppermint essence.

Hash Browns

Yields 12 hash browns
Preparation time 15 minutes
Cooking time 15 minutes
Degree of difficulty ☺☺

- 1 kg (2lbs) potatoes, peeled
- 1 large onion
- 1 teaspoon salt
- 1 teaspoon crumbled dried oregano, paprika or thyme
- 2 tablespoons crisp bacon bits
- 2 tablespoons cornstarch
- 1/2 cup unsalted butter
- 1/4 cup grated parmesan

1. Preheat the oven to 100°C (200°F). Cover an oven tray with a damp dishcloth. Grate all the potatoes and the onion, using the appropriate mixer utensil. Drain well on absorbent paper.
2. Place the potatoes and onion in a bowl and sprinkle with the herbs, cornstarch, salt and pepper. Melt the butter in a large non-stick skillet. Drop spoonfuls of the mixture into the skillet and press them with the back of an oiled spoon, so that they stick together. Fry for 5 minutes on each side.
3. Remove the hash browns to the dishcloth on the tray, sprinkle with the Parmesan and keep them warm in the oven until they are all ready.

Teddy bear fried eggs

Yields 6 portions
Preparation time 15 minutes
Degree of difficulty ☺

- 6 medium eggs
- 6 teddy bear egg molds
- 1 large griddle
- olive oil
- salt, pepper

1. It is easier to use a large griddle, on which you can cook all 6 eggs at once. Otherwise, cook them in a skillet, using as many molds as will fit inside it.
2. Coat the inside of the molds and the part that touches the frying plate with oil, using a brush. Break an egg into each mold and season with a little salt and pepper. Fry for 5-6 minutes, until the yolks set.
3. Transfer the eggs to plates using a metal spatula, and serve them with toast, ketchup and hash browns. If you like, add a few slices of grilled bacon, which children love.

Teddy Bear Pancakes with honey

Yields 10 pancakes
Preparation time 15 minutes
Cooking time 25 minutes
Degree of difficulty ☺☺

- 1 egg
- 1 cup buttermilk
- 2 tablespoons melted butter
- 1 cup all-purpose flour
- 1 tablespoon sugar
- 1 teaspoon baking powder
- 1/2 teaspoon bicarbonate of soda
- 1/2 teaspoon salt

1. Beat the egg lightly with a fork in a large bowl, and then add the rest of the ingredients. Beat with a hand mixer to form a smooth batter.
2. Butter the bottom of a non-stick skillet and heat it over high heat. Place 2 or 3 teddy bear molds into the skillet, having first dipped them into a shallow plate of oil. Place 1 tablespoon of the batter into each mold, and spread it with the back of a well-oiled spoon, so that the whole bottom of the mold is covered. Cook the pancakes for 2-3 minutes. Alternatively use a non-stick griddle.
3. As soon as each pancake rises, and before the bubbles on the surface burst, remove the metal mold, turn over the pancake and fry it until golden brown.
4. Make pretty mounds of hot pancakes spread with butter. Drizzle with honey or maple syrup and serve immediately.

Chocolate Thick-shakes

Yields 8-10 shakes
Preparation time 10 minutes
Degree of difficulty ☺

- 6 tablespoons chocolate powder
- 3 tablespoons chocolate syrup
- 6 cups cold milk
- 12 scoops chocolate ice cream
- pink or chocolate sprinkles

1. Beat all the ingredients, except the sprinkles, together in a blender, to form a smooth and thick chocolate mixture. Share it out into tall glasses and serve with pink sprinkles on top. For a thicker drink, add more scoops of ice cream.

Yields 30 sandwich cookies
Preparation time 1 hour
Baking time 10 minutes (200°C/400°F)
Degree of difficulty ☺☺

For the cookie dough
- 1 cup unsalted butter
- 1 cup icing sugar
- 1 cup plain flour
- 2 cups self-raising flour
- 2 teaspoons vanilla extract
- 6 tablespoons milk

For the fondant icing filling
- 1 egg white from a large egg
- 2 cups icing sugar
- a few drops of vanilla, peppermint or
  strawberry essence
- 1 egg white for coating the cookies
- glittering sugar in various colors,
  for sprinkling

Yields 4-6 glasses of milk shake
Preparation time 15 minutes
<u>Cooking for kids</u>

- 1/3 cup water
- 1/2 cup sugar
- 1 vanilla pod or 1 teaspoon vanilla powder
- 2 cups cold milk
- 8 scoops vanilla ice cream
  (around 1 kg/2lbs ice cream)

Yields 8 glasses of milk shake
Preparation time 10 minutes
Degree of difficulty ☺
<u>Cooking for kids</u>

- 4 bananas, not too soft
- 1/4 cup freshly squeezed lemon juice
- 3 tablespoons honey
- 2 cups milk
- 500g (1lb) vanilla ice cream

Yields 20-24 cookies
Preparation time 30 minutes
Baking time 10 minutes (180°C/360°F)
Degree of difficulty ☺☺

- 1 recipe butterfly cookie dough
  (recipe on page 89)
- a few drops red and blue food coloring
- 25 cookie sticks
- 1 egg white, lightly beaten
- glittering white sugar

Cream-filled vanilla cookies

1. Cream the butter with the sugar in the mixer, at medium speed for approximately 10 minutes, until white and fluffy. Sift the flour and add to the mixture. Add the vanilla and the milk and mix to form a soft and elastic dough. Do not knead the dough too much. Roll it out with a rolling pin into a thin sheet, between two pieces of non-stick paper. If the dough is too soft, refrigerate it for a while. If you like, add 100g (4oz) melted chocolate to the dough, to make chocolate cookies.
2. Cut cookies out of the dough using a round or square serrated pastry cutter (diameter: 4 cm/ 1.5 in). Make a design on the surface using the prongs of a fork. Arrange on a baking tray lined with non-stick paper. Bake at 200°C (400°F) for 10-12 minutes. Remove the cookies from the oven and let them cool on a rack. Prepare the icing. Beat the egg white with a hand mixer until foamy. Add the icing sugar gradually, beating constantly at low speed, until the icing has a thick, paste-like texture. Pour it onto a surface sprinkled with icing sugar and knead with the icing sugar until it sticks no longer to your hands.
3. Divide the fondant icing into three parts and place each one into a plastic food bag. Put the vanilla essence and a few drops of blue food coloring into one bag, peppermint essence and green food coloring in the second, and strawberry essence and red food coloring in the third. Close the bags and knead each piece of icing, until it is uniformly colored and scented. Using the bags will keep your hands from getting stained. Join together pairs of cookies using small balls of the colored icing. Press down so that the three layers stick together. Coat the cookies with a little egg white and sprinkle with glittering sugar in any color you like.

Real Vanilla Milk Shake

1. Boil the water with the sugar and the vanilla pod, split, to form runny syrup. Remove from the heat and take out the vanilla pod or add and stir in the vanilla powder, and let the mixture cool. Transfer to the blender, add the milk and ice cream and beat until soft. Pour into frozen glasses and serve immediately.

Old-fashioned Banana Milk Shake

1. Peel the bananas and put them in the blender, together with the lemon juice, honey and a little milk. Pulp the mixture. Add the remaining milk and beat until frothy. Pour into tall glasses and serve with scoops of soft vanilla ice cream.
2. Alternatively, replace the bananas with peeled peaches or canned peaches, or with 1 cup strawberries or kiwi, which kids love.

Fantasy Pinwheel Cookies

1. Prepare the dough according to the recipe. Divide the dough into three parts, and color two of them with a few drops of red and blue food coloring respectively. Roll out the white dough part onto non-stick oven paper, to form a large, thin rectangle. Do the same with the pink and blue dough on separate pieces of non-stick paper. Lift the blue sheet and place it over the white, then remove the paper. Carefully place the pink dough sheet over the blue and remove the paper. Press down to join the sheets and roll them into a tight roll.
2. Cut 3mm (0.1in) slices off the roll and arrange them on an unbuttered baking tray. Insert an oven-safe lollipop stick into the center of each wheel cookie and place the rack in the oven. You can also use the special pinwheel cookie molds that have special sockets for the lollipop sticks. Bake in a preheated oven for 10-12 minutes at 180°C (360°F). Remove to another baking tray and let cool before decorating. Coat the cookies with a little egg white, using a brush, and sprinkle with white glittering sugar.

Blue Dream Birthday Cake

Yields 20 portions
Preparation time 1 hour
Baking time 1 hour 10 minutes for the cake and
45 minutes for small cakes (180°C/360°F)
Suitable for freezing (final stage)
Degree of difficulty ☺☺

- 2 recipes very rich, very dark chocolate cake
  (recipe on page 23) or
  2 recipes blue sponge cake
  (Stars 'n' Bangles cake, recipe on page 107)
- 1 deep round 26-cm (10in) baking tin
- 1 jumbo muffin tray
- 6 white paper cupcakes for jumbo muffins

for the white chocolate filling
- 300g (12oz) white chocolate
- 3 tablespoons corn syrup (glucose)
- 3 tablespoons milk
- 3 egg yolks
- 2 tablespoons unsalted butter
- 2 cups whipping cream
- 1/2 sachet (20g or 1½ tablespoons)
  instant vanilla pudding
- 200g (8oz) sliced roasted almonds

for decorating
- pastry cutters for cake designs
- 1 tube white icing
- 2 tubes violet icing
- 2 recipes blue icing (recipe below)

1. Butter and flour the round baking tin. Line the jumbo muffin tray with the paper cupcakes. Prepare the two recipes of chocolate cake or blue sponge cake and pour the mixture into the muffin cases and buttered baking tin, filling 2/3 of each.

2. Bake the cake separately for 1 hour 10 minutes and the muffins for 45 minutes, at 180°C (360°F). Remove the cake from the oven, overturn it onto a rack and let it cool. Remove the muffins from the tray.

3. Prepare the filling. Place the chocolate, milk and corn syrup in a small saucepan or double boiler, and stir over low heat, until the chocolate melts. Blend in the egg yolks. Add the butter and stir until it melts and is incorporated in the white chocolate mixture. Remove the mixture from the heat and let cool. Beat the cream and instant vanilla pudding in the mixer until set. Add the chocolate mixture to the custard, a little at a time and continue to beat at low speed, until all the ingredients join to form a smooth and shiny cream.

4. Divide the cake into three layers. Place one layer on a serving stem platter. Spread half the cream on the first layer and sprinkle with half the roasted almonds. Cover with the second layer and spread over the rest of the cream and the remaining almonds. Place the third layer carefully over the cream. For ease, you can also assemble the cake inside a round metal ring. Cover the entire cake with blue icing, spreading it carefully with a metal spatula to make it smooth. Use any leftover icing to garnish the muffins and to pipe even rosettes around the cake. Press the pastry cutters for cake designs into the icing to leave pretty shapes. Pipe white icing around the shapes. Using violet icing, design a pretty lilac branch on the top of the cake. Also, design flowers on the muffins using colored icing. Keep the cake in the refrigerator until serving time. Will keep fresh for 2 days.

Blue icing

Yields 1 recipe
Preparation time 15 minutes
Degree of difficulty ☺

- 1 cup unsalted butter
- 400g (16oz) cream cheese, softened
- 5-6 cups icing sugar
- 2 teaspoons vanilla extract
- 4-6 tablespoons milk
- a few drops blue food coloring

1. Beat the butter in the mixer at medium speed, together with 1 cup of the sugar, until soft and creamy. Don't beat at high speed, otherwise the butter will curdle. Add the cream cheese and beat to incorporate. Add the rest of the icing sugar and vanilla, and incorporate in the mixture.

2. Add as much milk as necessary, to give the icing the right texture and render it smooth and soft. Stir in the blue food coloring, to achieve the desired color. If you like, you can use red, green or yellow food coloring to make pink, turquoise or pale yellow icing.

Teddy Bear Sandwiches

Yields 12 small sandwiches
Preparation time several hours
Baking time 30 minutes (200°C/400°F)
Degree of difficulty ☺☺☺

for the bread dough
- 3½ - 4 cups all-purpose flour
- 1 tablespoon dry yeast
- 1 teaspoon salt
- 3 tablespoons honey
- 3 tablespoons olive oil
- 1½ cups lukewarm water (40°C/80°F)

for the sandwiches
- mayonnaise or soft butter for spreading
- tender lettuce hearts
- 12 slices ham
- 12 slices cheese

1. Mix 3½ cups of the flour with the yeast and salt in the mixer bowl. Make a hole in the center and pour in the honey and oil. Add the water and mix with the dough hook, at low speed initially and then at high speed, to make a smooth and elastic dough. Add the remaining flour if necessary, so that the dough doesn't stick to the hook or the sides of the bowl.

2. Transfer the dough to a well-oiled bowl, cover with plastic wrap and let stand for 1 hour in a warm and humid place, until double in volume. Flour your hands, then cut and divide the dough into 12 sections and knead into small round balls. Arrange in an oiled baking pan, cover with plastic wrap and let rise for another 30 minutes.

3. Butter two teddy bear mold trays well and press each ball of dough down to fill the holes. Cover the dough in the trays with a dishcloth and let stand for 1 hour, until it doubles in volume.

4. Bake at 200°C (400°F) for 25-30 minutes, until golden brown. Serve the bread on the same day or wrap in plastic wrap and store in the freezer.

5. To make the sandwiches, cut the teddy bear rolls in two lengthways using a sharp knife. Spread with mayonnaise or soft butter and fill with lettuce, ham and cheese.

Easy solution: If you like, you can use store-bought refrigerator dough for white bread rolls. Two pieces of dough will fill 1 teddy bear mold. For 6 teddy bears you will need 2 boxes of dough (six rolls each). Knead two pieces of dough together and press to fill the teddy bear mold. When all the holes in the tray are full, cover the tray with a dishcloth and let the dough rise to cover the entire mold. Bake at 200°C (400°F), for 25 minutes.

Strawberry Pizza

Yields 12 portions
Preparation time 30 minutes
Baking time 25 minutes (180°C/360°F)
Degree of difficulty ☺☺

for the sweet dough
- 3 cups all-purpose flour
- 1 teaspoon powdered yeast
- 2 teaspoons vanilla powder
- 1/4 cup caster sugar
- 2/3 cup yogurt
- 2/3 cup warm milk
- 3 tablespoons melted butter

for the filling
- 1 cup strawberry jam
- 1/2 cup sliced roasted almonds
- 300g (12oz) fresh strawberries
- 1/2 cup small white marshmallows
- 1/2 cup chocolate chips
- 100g (4oz) white chocolate

1. Beat all the ingredients together, until the dough forms a ball around the dough hook. Continue beating for another 5 minutes, at low speed, until you obtain a soft and smooth dough.
2. Oil a large bowl well and place the dough inside it. Brush the surface with a little oil and cover with plastic wrap. Let the dough stand for 1 hour, until double in volume.
3. Press the risen dough down to let the air out, and place it in a well-buttered 30-cm (12in) pie pan. Press down to cover the bottom and sides.
4. Spread a thick layer of jam over the dough, leaving a 2-cm (1 in) gap round the sides. Sprinkle with sliced almonds. Wash, clean and slice the strawberries. Arrange the strawberries and marshmallows over the almonds. Sprinkle with the chocolate chips and grate the white chocolate to form shavings over the pizza. If you like, coat the sides of the pizza with a little egg yolk, for a nicer golden brown color. Bake the pizza at 180°C (360°F) for 20-25 minutes, until the dough at the sides is golden brown.

Roasted Almonds

To roast the almonds, line a baking pan with non-stick paper and arrange slices of blanched almonds on it. Bake at 180°C (360°F) for 10 minutes. Be careful not to burn them.

Dalmatian Brownies

**Yields 6, 7-cm (3-in) Dalmatians or
9 square pieces**
Baking time 30 minutes (180°C/360°F)
<u>Suitable for freezing</u>
Degree of difficulty ☺

- 1/4 cup unsalted butter
- 200g (7oz) white chocolate
- 1/2 cup chocolate chips
- 2 large eggs
- 1/2 cup caster sugar
- 2 teaspoons vanilla essence
- 1 cup cake flour plus 2 tablespoons extra
- 1/2 teaspoon baking powder

1. Melt the butter and half the white chocolate in a large saucepan. Chop up the remaining chocolate, mix it with the chocolate chips and 2 tablespoons flour, and set aside.

2. Remove the saucepan from the heat, add and mix in the sugar, eggs and vanilla, which you have previously beaten together. Sift the flour with the baking powder and a pinch of salt, and add to the mixture. Mix in with the rest of the ingredients to form smooth dough.

3. Fold in the chocolate pieces. Pour the mixture into a round 22-cm (9-in) baking pan, well buttered and lined with non-stick oven paper, also greased. Bake the mixture in the center of the oven, at 180°C (360°F) for 30 minutes. Remove from the oven and overturn on a rack spread with non-stick paper and sprinkled with icing sugar. Let cool for 15 minutes and cut out Dalmatian puppies with pastry cutters.

4. For teddy bear brownies, prepare and bake your favorite brownie recipe and cut out pretty teddy bears with metal pastry cutters.

Super Chocolate Sponge Cake

For a 27-30 cm (11-12 in) birthday cake
Baking time 30-35 minutes (180°C/360°F)
Degree of difficulty ☺

- 2 cups sugar
- 2 cups self-raising flour
- 1 cup unsweetened cocoa
- 1 teaspoon bicarbonate of soda
- 1/2 teaspoon vanilla
- 1/4 teaspoon salt
- 2 eggs
- 2/3 cup milk
- 1 teaspoon vanilla extract
- 1/2 cup corn oil
- 2/3 cup boiling water

1. Place all the ingredients, except the boiling water, in the mixer bowl, and beat for 2 minutes. Add the water and beat at low speed to incorporate in the dough. Butter and flour two round sponge cake tins well, or line them with non-stick paper, also buttered. Divide the dough into the tins and bake separately at 180°C (360°F) for 30-35 minutes.

2. For an easy super chocolate birthday cake, prepare 1 recipe easy chocolate icing (page 29). Join the two sponge cake layers with half the icing and cover the cake with the other half. Keep refrigerated.

Chocolate Mousse Heart Cake

Yields 20 portions
Preparation time 2 hours
<u>Suitable for freezing (final stage)</u>
Degree of difficulty ☺☺

for the chocolate sponge
- 4 eggs
- 1 cup sugar
- 2/3 cup self-raising flour
- 1/2 cup unsweetened cocoa
- 1 teaspoon vanilla extract
- 3 tablespoons melted unsalted butter

for the truffle mousse filling
- 1 tablespoon gelatine powder
- 1 cup milk
- 1/2 cup unsalted butter
- 1/2 cup unsweetened cocoa
- 250g (8oz) pieces of dark chocolate
- 2 tablespoons Kahlua liqueur
- 2 egg whites
- 1/3 cup icing sugar
- 1 cup double cream
- 2 cups whipped cream, for garnishing
- blue or pink sprinkles

1. Prepare the sponge cake. Beat the eggs and sugar in the mixer at high speed, until set and double in volume. Mix the flour with the cocoa and a little vanilla and sift the mixture a little at a time into the bowl with the eggs, continuing to beat at very low speed, or mixing lightly with a spatula to make a smooth mixture. Take care not to deflate the eggs. Add the melted butter and mix in gently.

2. Pour the mixture into a buttered and floured heart-shaped cake tin. Bake the sponge cake at 180°C (360°F) for 35 minutes or until a skewer comes out clean. Remove from the oven, overturn onto a rack spread with non-stick oven paper, sprinkled with icing sugar, and let cool.

3. Prepare the filling. Dissolve the gelatine in the milk and let stand for 10 minutes. Melt the butter in a large saucepan. Add and mix in the cocoa. Add the gelatine and milk and mix in, until the mixture is well heated and the gelatine dissolves. Add the pieces of chocolate and mix over low heat, until melted.

4. Remove the chocolate mixture from the heat, pour and mix in the liqueur and let cool. Beat the egg whites and sugar in the mixer, to make a soft meringue. Beat the cream with 1 teaspoon vanilla powder, until set. Mix the chocolate mixture with the beaten cream first, and then fold in the meringue.

5. Cut the heart-shaped sponge cake into 2 layers and join them with half the chocolate mousse. Garnish the surface with the remaining chocolate mousse and the whipped cream, using a piping bag. Sprinkle over the pink or blue chocolate sprinkles. Refrigerate the cake for at least 4 hours or overnight, until set, or store it for a short while in the freezer, in a cake box.

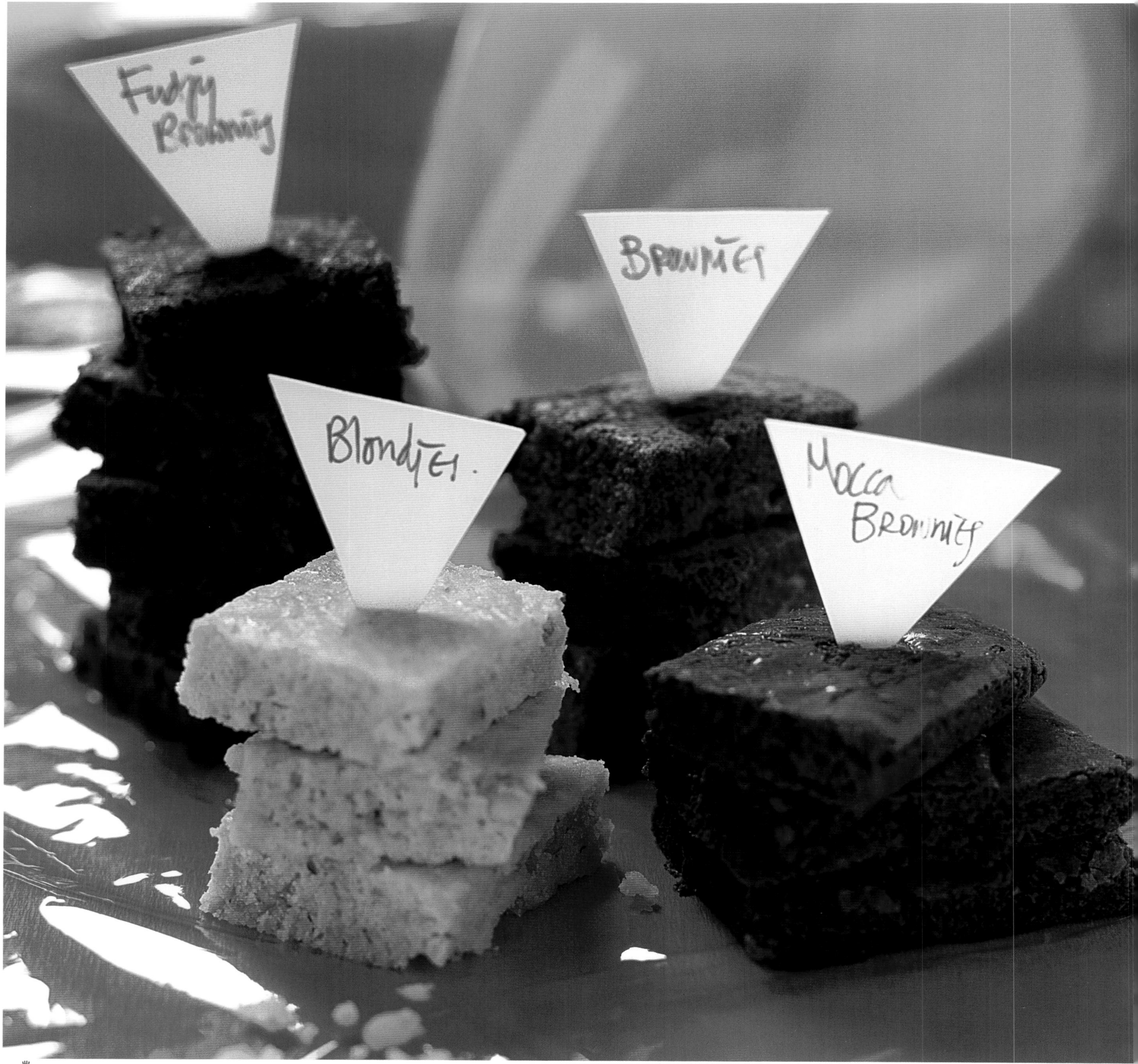
Fudgy Brownies
Brownies
Blondies.
Mocca Brownies

Each recipe yields 9 brownies
Preparation time 20 minutes
Baking time 30 minutes (180°C/360°F)
<u>Suitable for freezing</u>
Degree of difficulty ☺☺

- 150g (6oz) chocolate chips, melted
- 1/4 cup (1/2 stick) unsalted butter, soft
- 2/3 cup caster sugar
- 2 large eggs
- 2 teaspoons vanilla essence
- 1/4 cup milk
- 2/3 cup cake flour, not self-raising
- 1 teaspoon baking powder
- a little salt

1. Butter a square 22x22 cm (9x9 in) baking pan well. Line the bottom with non-stick oven paper and butter again.
2. Beat the butter and sugar in the mixer until white and creamy. Add the eggs, vanilla, and milk and beat for 1 minute to incorporate. Add the melted chocolate and beat for a while, to obtain a smooth mixture.
3. Sift the flour with the baking powder and salt into the bowl, and beat for another minute. Pour the mixture into the baking pan and bake on the oven's middle rack at 180°C (360°F) for 25-30 minutes, or until a skewer comes out clean. When you remove the pan from the oven, separate the cake from the sides using a knife, and overturn onto a surface spread with non-stick paper and sprinkled with icing sugar. Remove the paper and cut the brownies into square pieces. Serve on the same day, or place in food bags when cold and store in the freezer.

Mocca Brownies

- 1/2 cup chocolate chips
- 2/3 cup unsalted butter
- 1/3 cup unsweetened cocoa
- 2 tablespoons instant coffee
- 1 cup caster sugar
- 1/4 teaspoon salt
- 1 teaspoon vanilla essence
- 2 large eggs
- 3/4 cup self-raising flour

1. Butter a square 22x22 cm (9x9 in) baking pan well. Line the bottom with non-stick oven paper and butter again.
2. Melt the chocolate with the butter, cocoa and instant coffee in a large saucepan. Remove from the heat, and when slightly cool, add and mix in the sugar, salt and vanilla. Add the eggs and beat to incorporate. Stir in the flour.
3. Pour the batter into the baking pan and bake on the oven's middle shelf at 180°C (360°F) for 30 minutes, or until a skewer comes out almost clean. When you remove the pan from the oven, separate the cake from the sides using a knife, and overturn onto a surface spread with non-stick paper and sprinkled with icing sugar. Remove the paper and when the cake is cool, cut the brownies into square pieces. Serve on the same day, or place in food bags and store in the freezer.

Fudgy Brownies

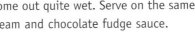

- 200g (7oz) chocolate chips
- 2 tablespoons corn syrup
- 2/3 cup unsalted butter
- 2 teaspoons vanilla essence
- a little salt
- 3 large eggs
- 2/3 cup self-raising flour

1. Follow the same procedure as in "Mocca Brownies". Melt the corn syrup and brown sugar together with the butter and chocolate. After 30 minutes baking time, when the brownies are ready, a skewer will come out quite wet. Serve on the same day, or place in food bags and store in the freezer. Serve with scoops of vanilla ice cream and chocolate fudge sauce.

Blondies

- 1/2 cup unsalted butter
- 1 cup light brown sugar
- 1 tablespoon corn syrup
- 2 large eggs and 1 yolk
- a little salt
- 1½ teaspoons vanilla essence
- 1¼ cups all-purpose flour
- 1/2 teaspoon baking powder
- 1/2 cup coarsely ground hazelnuts or roasted almonds

1. Butter a square 22x22 cm (9x9 in) baking pan well. Line the bottom with non-stick oven paper and butter again.
2. Melt the butter, light brown sugar and corn syrup in a large saucepan over medium heat, until the sugar dissolves completely. Remove from the heat, and when cool, add and mix in the eggs, egg yolk, salt and vanilla. Add the flour, baking powder and hazelnuts and mix to incorporate.
3. Pour the batter into the prepared baking pan and bake on the oven's middle shelf at 180°C (360°F) for 30 minutes, or until a skewer comes out almost clean. When you remove the pan from the oven, separate the cake from the sides using a knife, and overturn onto a surface spread with non-stick paper and sprinkled with icing sugar. Remove the paper and when the cake is cold, cut the brownies into square pieces. Serve on the same day, or place in food bags and store in the freezer.

Preparation time 20 minutes
Refrigeration time 2 hours
<u>Cooking for children</u>

- 1 lb (500g) cooking chocolate
- 8 oz (250g) white and pink marshmallows or
  1 cup chopped dried candied fruits
- 1 cup coarsely ground cashews or hazelnuts or
  roasted and caramelized almonds

1. Make your own chocolate bar by combining melted chocolate with various nuts, marshmallows, dried fruits or liqueur.

2. Melt the chocolate. Choose the best quality you can obtain. In order to be sure of the quality, select the chocolate with the highest cocoa solids content. Add 1 teaspoon of your favorite essence to the melted chocolate (strawberry, vanilla, bitter almond, orange or peppermint) or a fruit-scented liqueur, according to your taste.

3. Line a small square (22x22cm/9x9 in) baking pan with non-stick oven paper, and pour in half of the melted chocolate, enough to cover the bottom in a thin layer.

4. Sprinkle over the white and pink marshmallows or dried candied fruits, such as sultanas, chopped dried plums, apricots or figs. Also, add your favorite nuts here and there on the melted chocolate. Pour over the rest of the chocolate and place the pan in the refrigerator until the chocolate sets completely, about 2 hours.

5. Remove the pan from the refrigerator, overturn it onto the worktop and cut the chocolate bar in pieces, using a sharp knife. Kids love chocolate with marshmallows and cashew nuts. Try it!

6. You can place the pieces in small transparent bags, tie them with colorful bows and hand them out to the children at the end of the party.

Crazy for chocolate Angel Food cake

Yields 16 portions
Preparation time 20 minutes
Baking time 40 minutes (180°C/360°F)
Suitable for freezing (final stage)
Degree of difficulty ☺☺

- 1/3 cup unsweetened cocoa
- 1/3 cup self-raising flour
- 1½ cups sugar
- a little salt
- 12 egg whites
- 1 tablespoon lemon juice or
  1 teaspoon cream of tartar
- 1 teaspoon vanilla essence
- 1/2 teaspoon bitter almond extract
- 100g (4oz) chocolate flakes

1. Pulse the cocoa, flour, half the sugar and the salt in the blender until pulverized.
2. Beat the egg whites with the lemon juice or cream of tartar and the essences in the mixer, until frothy. Add half the remaining sugar and beat for approximately 10 minutes to form a soft meringue. Add the remaining sugar and continue beating to form a stiff meringue.
3. Stop beating and sift the solid ingredients mixture into the egg whites, a little at a time. Stir gently with a spatula after each addition, to mix the flour in but not deflate the mixture. If the mixture doesn't fit in the mixer bowl, divide it in two. Finally, add the chocolate flakes to the mixture and fold in gently.
4. Pour spoonfuls of the mixture into an unbuttered angel food cake mold. Bake on the lower oven shelf at 180°C (360°F) for 35-40 minutes. Remove from the oven, overturn in the mold, and stand on the mold's feet; cool for 1 hour.
5. Use a knife to separate the cake from the sides of the mold and remove to a platter. At this stage, you can wrap the cake in plastic wrap and freeze it for up to 2 months. Once defrosted, cut into 2 layers and join with 2/3 of the pink icing. Garnish the cake surface with the rest of the pink icing, using a piping bag, and store in the refrigerator until serving time.
6. Prepare pink and chocolate lollipops using candy melts, in ballet-related shapes, and stick them onto the cake. Your young guests will be impressed. Lollipop recipe on page 127 (rose lollipops).

Pink Frosting

- 1 cup unsalted butter or
  white vegetable shortening
- 1 cup cream cheese, softened
- 4 cups icing sugar
- 1 teaspoon strawberry essence
- a few drops red food coloring

1. Beat all the ingredients together in the mixer, at medium speed, to form a soft and fluffy icing. If the icing is too thick, add 2-3 tablespoons milk. Use immediately or place in a piping bag and store in the refrigerator.

Shortbread Teddy Bear

Yields 10 portions
Preparation time 20 minutes
Baking time 40 minutes (150°C/300°F)
Degree of difficulty ☺☺

- 1 cup unsalted butter
- 2/3 cup caster sugar
- 125g (5oz) dark baking chocolate
- 2½ - 2²/₃ cups soft flour
- a pinch of salt

1. Cream the butter and sugar in the mixer, at medium speed, until white. Meanwhile, melt the chocolate over very low heat or in a double boiler.

2. Add the melted chocolate to the beaten butter and beat to form a uniform chocolate mixture. Pour in the flour immediately and knead the mixture softly to form smooth dough that doesn't stick to your hands. Do not knead the mixture too much or the biscuit will turn out hard.

3. Butter a teddy bear-shaped shortbread cookie pan and line with buttered non-stick paper. Roll out the dough on a pastry cloth, using a rolling pin covered with the same material, to make a sheet larger than the diameter of the pan. Overturn the sheet into the pan, aided by the pastry cloth, and cut the pieces overhanging the sides carefully.

4. Bake the shortbread at 150°C (300°F) for 40 minutes. Let cool for 15 minutes and overturn onto a rack lined with parchment paper. At this stage, and while the cookie is still soft, you can use a knife to score pieces, without separating them, so that it will be easier to cut when served. Let the shortbread cool completely before garnishing. The longer it stands, the harder it gets. Garnish with soft chocolate icing (recipe on page 179) or store-bought chocolate icing and colored candy.

Wow! Chocolate hazelnut brownies

Yields 50 brownies
Preparation time 20 minutes
Baking time 30-35 minutes
(170°C/340°F)
Suitable for freezing (final stage)
Degree of difficulty ☺☺

- 250g (8oz) dark baking chocolate
- 1 cup (2 sticks) unsalted butter
- 1/2 cup milk
- 2/3 cup caster sugar
- 2/3 cup brown sugar
- 2 teaspoons vanilla powder
- 4 eggs
- 1½ cups self-raising flour
- 1 cup coarsely ground hazelnuts
- 1 square 28-cm (11-in) baking pan

for the white filling
- 400g (14oz) cream cheese, softened
- 1 cup (2 sticks) unsalted butter
- 3 cups icing sugar
- 3 tablespoons milk
- 2 teaspoons vanilla essence

for the shiny chocolate icing
- 1/2 cup (1 stick) unsalted butter,
  melted and mixed with
  1/3 cup unsweetened cocoa
- 2 tablespoons light corn syrup
- 2 cups double cream
- 400g (14oz) dark baking chocolate
- 1 cup white mini marshmallows

1. Prepare the brownie mixture. Place the first 5 ingredients in a large saucepan and mix to form a smooth, uniform mixture.

2. Remove the chocolate mixture from the heat and let cool slightly. Add the vanilla, eggs, flour and hazelnuts and mix well with a spoon. Pour the mixture into a square 28x28cm (10X10in) buttered baking pan, and bake at 175°C (350°F) for 30-35 minutes.

3. Remove the cake from the oven and let cool in the pan. Beat all the ingredients for the white icing in the blender and pour over the cake in the pan. Refrigerate for 1 hour to set.

4. Mix the melted butter with the cocoa and corn syrup. Heat the cream in a small saucepan. Add the chocolate pieces, marshmallows and melted butter. Stir over medium heat, to form a smooth icing. Pour the chocolate icing over the white icing in the pan. Return the brownies to the refrigerator and let the icing set. Serve cut in square pieces. Children and adults will adore this dessert. The brownies are ideal accompaniments for coffee. Will keep for 5 days in the refrigerator and for several weeks in the freezer.

Garden Parties!

Little fairies' spring party...74 American Dream, pool party or beach party...92 "Make food, not war" hippie party...110 Picnic for young sports fans...128 August birthday at the summerhouse...138

Little fairies' spring party

(FOR GIRLS 👧 AGED 1 AND ABOVE)

Beautiful spring brings with it a plethora of celebrations, and the mild weather makes it an ideal time for a party in the garden, which children will love. Organize a dream butterfly party, "dressed" in pink, with suitable garden decorations, to celebrate your baby's first birthday, a precious four-year-old princess, or the romantic young lady turning sixteen.

Buy pink organza ribbons to decorate the cake with and to hang as decorations from the garden's trees. The house doorway can also be decorated with a lantern tied with pink ribbons and some pink cardboard announcing the party. Another smart idea is to include the name of the young hostess, who will be the honored person at the party. Draw pretty butterflies on the cardboard, and write your message with a pink felt-tip. Attach the cardboard to a piece of wood, so that you can plant it in a flowerpot at the entrance, or tie it to the door with ribbons. Prepare original butterfly invitations. Fold a few sheets of yellow, blue and pink A4 cardboard in two and cut them into large butterflies. Stick multi-colored sequins or confetti on the outside, and write the party message on the inside.

For your party table, you can make a pretty tablecloth by sewing square pieces of bright-colored (fuchsia, yellow, purple, orange) thin cotton cloth together, to form an oblong tablecloth for your garden table. Using an indelible marker, write messages on the tablecloth together with the children. Don't forget that this party is for the children's amusement, and what will make them happiest is participating in every stage, even in the preparations. A successful children's party doesn't only depend on the effort or the money spent, so there is no need to resort to expensive solutions in order to impress your guests. Instead, improvise and let your imagination run wild when decorating the garden, the table and the food.

Cutting the cake and blowing out the candles is the apex of the party. Make sure you cut the cake near the middle of the party, so that all the guests are present, and the children are still energetic. A three-tiered cake is an amazing spectacle for the young guests, and is a great idea to make your child feel even more special, as she will

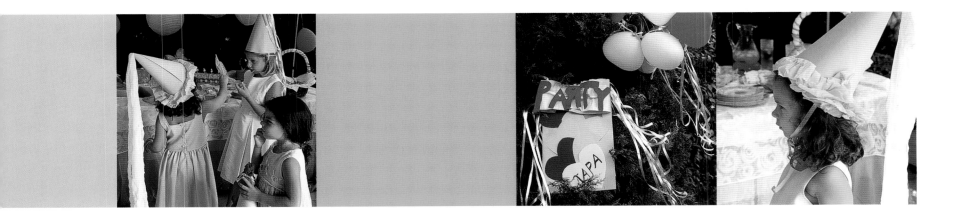

have to climb up high to blow out the candles. Photographs and a video are a must, as they will make your daughter feel like a real princess.

Children love popcorn, and they will love it even more if it is served in white bags with their names on. Paint the bags together with your child, and write the names of the guests on them. Popcorn and milkshakes can be served at the end of the party.

An original idea is to decorate the milkshake straws with cardboard butterflies cut out using a pair of jagged scissors. Stick the butterflies halfway up the pink straws.

At the end of the party, you can give the young guests butterfly cookies in pretty boxes. The children and their mothers will be thrilled to have a homemade dessert to take to school with them the next day. Also share out the party decorations, the paper butterflies and fairy hats.

Don't forget, if your daughter's guests are from school, give her the party photographs to take to school and show them to her schoolmates. Have a chat with the mothers about the photos of their sweet children that they wish to order.

FOOD & SWEETS FOR THE KIDS

✿ Chicken pies

✿ Butterfly tostadas

✿ Pink farfalle pasta with peppers

✿ Pink yogurt smoothies

✿ Butterfly rosettes

✿ Jumbo butterfly muffins

✿ Dream butterfly cake

✿ Pink popcorn

✿ Butterfly cookies

✿ Carousel cake

FOOD & SWEETS FOR MOMMIES AND DADDIES

✿ Butterfly tostadas

✿ Butterfly panini contadino

✿ Chicken strudel with peppers and brie

✿ Pink farfalle pasta with peppers

✿ Butterfly sponge cake muffins

✿ Papillon choux à la crème

✿ "Strawberries and cream" butterfly cake

Party Diary

Genova's Party

One month to two weeks in advance

1. Decide on the date of the party. Even though it is nice to have the party on the actual birthday, it is better if the young guests are rested, and don't have school or studying to do. The best days and times for a children's party are Saturday afternoon or Sunday morning. As the party will be held in the garden, make sure you listen to the weather reports well in advance. It is a good idea to have an alternative solution, such as gathering the children somewhere in the house if the weather turns bad.

2. Prepare the invitations and share them out or send them to the guests. Find out over the phone how many adults and children plan to attend.

3. Arrange the party decorations quite early on. Let your child help you make hats out of colored shiny cardboard, and stick on shapes, circles, stars or triangles cut out of different-colored paper. If you like, you can attach long ribbons or a scarf to the top of each hat. Cut butterflies out of pink cardboard and write each little guest's name on them, and attach them to each child's glass. Prepare the party notice to be hung at the entrance to the house or garden.

Two weeks to two days in advance

1. Prepare the Dream butterfly cake and the butterfly sponge cake muffins. Cover the cake with the Regalice, stick the glacé cherries on it, cover the cake with plastic wrap and store it in the freezer.

2. Bake the strawberry sponge for the cake, and, once cold, cover it and store it in the freezer. Make the jumbo muffins and store them, too, in the freezer.

3. Prepare the butterfly tortillas for the tostadas, and store them in the freezer. Instead of tortillas, you can use ready-made pitta bread cut into butterfly shapes with pastry cutters on the day before the party. Store them in an airtight cookie tin.

4. Prepare the chicken & pepper rolls and store them in the freezer. Prepare the tartlets, bake them, cover them, and store them in the freezer.

Two days in advance

1. Bake the choux and store them covered in plastic wrap.
2. Make the strawberry sauce for the butterfly cake.
3. Take the strawberry sponge out of the freezer and keep it in the refrigerator.
4. Whip the cream and store it covered in the refrigerator.
5. Marinate the chicken for the tostadas and store it in the fridge.
6. Bake the butterfly cookies.

The day before the party, in the morning

1. Assemble the butterfly choux, garnish and store them in the refrigerator, on a serving platter.

2. Prepare the butterfly cake with strawberry sauce, garnish it with the whipped cream and store it uncovered in the fridge.

3. Prepare the avocado sauce and the chicken stuffing for the tostadas; store them covered in the fridge. At this stage, marinate the pieces of tomato and pepper for the tostadas in a bowl, as well as the eggplant for the sandwiches.

The night before

1. Cut the bread and cheese for the sandwiches, cover them, and store the latter in the refrigerator.

2. Take the tartlets out of the freezer and defrost at room temperature. Prepare the chicken tartlet filling, cover it, and store it in the fridge.

3. Put the cookies that you plan to give to the guests in pretty boxes, and tie them with colored ribbons.

4. Decorate the jumbo butterfly muffins and store them at room temperature, covered with a cake bell.

5. Take the birthday cake out of the freezer and let it stand at room temperature for at least 6-7 hours.

In the morning of the party

1. Take the chicken rolls out of the freezer.

2. Assemble the miniature sandwiches and store them on a covered platter in the refrigerator. Fill the tartlets with the chicken mixture and arrange them on an oven dish. Store covered in the refrigerator.

3. Prepare the farfalle mixture and store it in the refrigerator.

4. Place all the ingredients on the butterfly-shaped tortillas or pitta bread and arrange them on a baking tray. Cover and store in the fridge until baking time, 15 minutes before serving.

5. Bake the chicken rolls and tartlets and keep them warm.

6. Boil the pasta and mix it with the pepper mixture you have already prepared. If you have help in the kitchen during the party, boil the farfalle just before serving.

During the party

1. Serve the butterfly cookies with coffee for the adults. If you like, you can prepare butterfly-shaped sugar cubes in special molds, and color them pink, to serve with the coffee (recipe on page 219).

2. Set up a donut maker somewhere in the garden, and fry the butterfly rosettes during the party. It's a good idea to get someone to help you with the frying. Sprinkle icing sugar over the rosettes and share them out to the young guests.

3. Prepare the smoothies and serve them to the children. Don't forget to give them their gifts at the end of the party.

Good Things for kids

Smoothies: Instead of the usual ice cream milk shakes, serve lighter and more healthy yogurt smoothies with strawberry sorbet.

Strawberry cake: Ideal for young friends who are not too fond of chocolate. Prepare a sweet surprise for all the kids, a delicious soft vanilla cake, filled with a sweet sauce made with their favorite fruit.

Pepperoni and pepper sauce for pasta: The children will benefit from all the vitamins in the peppers, without noticing it through the delight of the tasty pasta sauce. Farfalla in Italian means butterfly.

Butterfly cookies and jumbo muffins: Share them out to the kids at the end of the party. There is nothing better than a homemade snack to take to school with them the next day.

Crème Pâtissière

Yields 2 cups cream
Preparation time 40 minutes

- 1 cup sugar
- 6 egg yolks
- 1/3 cup cornstarch
- 2½ cups milk
- 3 tablespoons unsalted butter, chilled

1. Beat the egg yolks and the sugar in a large bowl, until stiff and lemon-colored. Add the flour and a little salt, sifting over the egg mixture, and stir to incorporate.

2. Boil the milk and add it a spoonful at a time to the egg yolk mixture, stirring briskly. Transfer the cream to a small saucepan with a heavy bottom and boil over low heat, stirring constantly, until set. The cream must simmer for 10-15 minutes so that it doesn't smell of flour. Remove from the heat, add and mix in the butter.

3. Cover with plastic wrap, stuck to the surface, and store in the refrigerator for up to 2 days. For a lighter filling, mix in 2 cups of whipped cream.

4. For chocolate cream, add 125g dark chocolate to the warm cream, and blend it in. For vanilla cream, add 1 vanilla pod, split lengthways, to the milk before you boil it.

Strawberry Sauce

Yields 4 cups sauce

- 4 cups strawberries, washed and cut in half
- 1½ cups sugar
- 4 tablespoons cornstarch
- 4 tablespoons lemon juice

1. Mix the strawberries, sugar, cornstarch and lemon juice in a saucepan. Simmer gently, stirring occasionally, until it sets to form a transparent, shiny sauce. Remove from the heat.

Carousel Cake (photograph on page 91)

Yields 1 oblong cake = 20 portions
Preparation time 1 hour
Baking time 40 minutes
Suitable for freezing (final stage)
Degree of difficulty ☺

- 1 recipe vanilla sponge cake (recipe on page 51)
- 1 oblong angel food cake mold
- 1/2 recipe mini meringues (recipe on page 190)
- blue and pink food coloring paste
- 2 recipes pink icing (recipe on page 69)
- carousel horse candles
- pink shiny sprinkles for decorating

1. Your cake can be pink, lilac, orange or yellow; color the icing and/or sponge cake with your favorite food coloring. Instead of horses, you can use any kind of decorative candle, such as teddy bears, ballerinas, computers, toy soldiers, musical notes, rackets, pussy cats or babies.

2. Butter the cake mold well, and line the bottom with non-stick oven paper. Prepare the sponge cake mix and pour it into the mold. Alternatively, make the cake with 2 boxes of white cake mix. Bake in a preheated oven at 180°C (360°F) for 35-40 minutes or 1 hour for the store-bought mix, until a skewer comes out clean. Remove the cake to a platter and when cold, divide into two layers with a sharp knife or cake separator.

3. Prepare the icing and fill the cake with half of it. Garnish the cake surface with the remaining icing. Sprinkle the cake with shiny sugar and stick your favorite candles into it.

4. Beat the meringue. Divide in two and color one part pink and the other blue. Fill two piping bags with the colored meringue and pipe mini rosettes onto a rack covered with non-stick paper. Bake the mini meringues for 1 hour at 90°C (180°F). Store in a cookie jar for decorating or use to decorate the cake.

Whipped Cream – Crème du Chantilly

Yields 4 cups cream (1 pound - 500g store-bought whipped cream)

- 2 cups (500 ml) whipping cream
- 1/2 cup icing sugar
- 1 teaspoon vanilla essence
- 1 sachet whipped cream thickener (optional) or
  1/2 teaspoon gelatine, dissolved in 1 teaspoon cold water

1. The cream you use must be chilled. Whip the cream with the icing sugar, vanilla and thickener or gelatine until it sets and forms a smooth, soft and light whipped cream. Do not over-whip the cream, as it will curdle. Store the whipped cream in the refrigerator, covered, until you want to use it. Whipped cream is very sensitive to heat; it turns soft. If the whipped cream goes soft, beat it again until stiff.

Dream Butterfly Cake

Yields 30 pieces
Preparation time 2 hours
Baking time 1 hour (180°C/360°F)
<u>Suitable for freezing (final stage)</u>
Degree of difficulty ☺☺☺☺

- 2 recipes chocolate sponge cake
  (page 65)
  or very rich cake (page 23) or
  2 boxes chocolate cake mix
- 2/3 cup raspberry jam
- 1 recipe truffle mousse filling
  (recipe on page 65)
- 1 recipe royal icing
  (recipe on page 167)
- 1 packet Regalice or
  1kg (2lbs) homemade sugar paste
  (recipe on page 113)

1. Prepare the sponge cake or the store-bought cake by following the instructions on the box. Pour the cake mix into a well-buttered round baking pan, 37 cm (14-in) in diameter. Bake the cake at 180°C (360°F), for 1 hour.

2. Remove from the oven and overturn onto a rack spread with non-stick paper and sprinkled with icing sugar, and let cool. Divide into two layers. Transfer one layer to a serving platter and spread with heated, melted raspberry jam. Spread the chocolate filling on top. Cover with the second layer and refrigerate the cake until the filling sets, around 1 hour. Remove the cake from the refrigerator and coat the entire surface with royal icing.

3. Prepare the Regalice and roll out a round sheet (diameter: 40cm/ 15in) with a rolling pin, on a work surface sprinkled with icing sugar. Make sure the rolling pin is also covered with icing sugar, so that the paste doesn't stick to it. Wrap the sheet around a long, thin rod, like material. Transfer it to the cake and unroll carefully, taking care not to tear the icing.

4. Cut off the pieces that are left around the cake and roll them into a long thin strip. Use to cover the sides of the cake. If you need to cover any imperfections, make pretty designs on the surface with royal icing, using a piping bag with a thin nozzle.

5. Stick 4 mini butterfly cakes to the top of the birthday cake, using a little royal icing. Tie a pretty pink ribbon around it, for decoration. Store in the refrigerator for 2 days, uncovered, or cover with plastic wrap and store in the freezer for up to 1 month.

Mini Butterfly Sponge Cakes

Yields 8 mini butterfly cakes
Preparation time 1 hour
Baking time 35 minutes (180°C/360°F)
<u>Suitable for freezing</u>
Degree of difficulty ☺☺

- 1 recipe vanilla sponge cake
  (recipe on page 51) or
  1 box white cake mix powder
- 1 recipe easy icing
  (recipe on page 29) or
  1 jar ready-made vanilla icing
  (14oz/ 400g)
- pink shiny sugar

1. Prepare the small recipe of sponge cake mix. If using ready-made cake mix, follow the instructions on the packet. Pour the batter into a well-buttered jellyroll pan spread with non-stick oven paper, also buttered. Bake at 180°C (360°F) for 35 minutes or until it separates from the walls of the pan.

2. Overturn onto a rack spread with non-stick paper, and let cool. When the sponge cake has cooled down, cut out butterfly shapes using a 10-cm (4-in) sandwich cutter.

3. Place the mini cakes onto a clean rack standing in a pan, so that the extra icing can drop into it. Prepare the icing and heat it over low heat or in a microwave oven for a few seconds, until liquid. Pour the icing over the mini cakes, spoonful by spoonful, until the surface is completely covered. Before the icing sets, sprinkle the shiny sugar over the cakes. Stand for 1 hour, until the icing has set completely.

Butterfly cake with strawberry sauce and whipped cream

Yields 20 portions
Preparation time 1 hour
Baking time 1 hour (180°C/360°F)
<u>Suitable for freezing (final stage)</u>
Degree of difficulty ☺☺☺

for the soft strawberry cake
- 3 cups self-raising flour
- 2 cups sugar
- 4 medium eggs
- 250g (8oz) soft margarine
- 1/3 cup milk
- 2 teaspoons strawberry essence
- a few drops red food coloring
- 2 teaspoons vanilla essence

for the filling
- 1½ cups strawberry sauce
  (recipe on page 77)
- 2 cups whipped cream
- 500g (1lb) ready-made royal icing or
  1kg (2lbs) whipped cream or
  2 recipes butter icing
  (recipe on page 179), for coating

1. Beat all the cake ingredients together at high speed in the mixer, for about 4 minutes. Pour the mixture into a 25-cm (10-in) butterfly mold, sprayed with butter. Bake the cake at 180°C (360°F) for about 1 hour 10 minutes.

2. Remove the cake from the oven, overturn on a rack and let cool. Cut the cake into three layers. Transfer the bottom layer to a platter, and coat with whipped cream. Cover with strawberry sauce, using a metal spatula. Repeat with the second layer and cover with the last layer. Place the cake in the refrigerator.

3. Prepare the royal icing and fill a large piping bag with a #789 nozzle. Cover the cake with icing, to shape the butterfly's wings and circumference. Sprinkle with a little red sugar and affix two small pieces of red wire with marshmallows attached, for the antennae. Store the cake uncovered in the refrigerator.

Panini Contadino

Yields 12 sandwiches
Preparation time 3 hours
Baking time for the eggplant 25 minutes
(180°C/360°F)
Degree of difficulty ☺☺

- 1 large eggplant, thinly sliced
- 1/2 teaspoon crumbled dried thyme, oregano
- 1/4 cup virgin olive oil
- 1/3 cup balsamic vinegar
- 24 slices brown sandwich bread
- 2/3 cup olive paste
- 24 arugula, watercress, rocket or spinach leaves
- 6 thin slices Parmiggiano Reggiano, cut in half
- 24 slices Milan salami

1. Sprinkle the eggplant slices with salt and let them drain for 2 hours. Rinse with plenty of cold water and press each slice between your palms, to remove excess water. Arrange in a buttered baking pan, sprinkle with thyme and oregano and drizzle with olive oil. Bake at 180°C (360°F) for 25 minutes. As soon as you remove the eggplant slices from the oven, pour over the vinegar and let cool. Cover and marinate in the refrigerator for a few hours.

2. Use butterfly-shaped pastry cutters to cut the sandwich bread on the day before, and store the slices in an airtight container. Wash the arugula, spinach or rocket thoroughly and dry on absorbent paper. Refrigerate.

3. Just before serving, drain the eggplant slices well. Spread olive paste on the slices of bread and divide the eggplant and other ingredients onto half the bread slices. Cover with the other half and serve the sandwiches immediately. For children, serve the sandwiches with fresh spinach leaves instead of arugula.

Butterfly Tostadas

Yields 12 tostadas
Preparation time 30 minutes
Cooking time 35 minutes + 10 minutes grilling
Degree of difficulty ☺☺☺

- 300g (12oz) chicken breast, boned and diced
- 1/2 cup freshly squeezed lemon juice
- 1/2 cup virgin olive oil
- 1 teaspoon oregano
- 1/2 cup finely chopped fresh ripe tomato, no juice
- 1/2 cup finely chopped red and green pepper
- 1 recipe tortilla dough (recipe on page 95)

for the sauce
- 3 tablespoons olive oil
- 1/2 onion, grated
- 2 cloves garlic, crushed
- 2 tablespoons Worcestershire sauce
- 2 tablespoons ketchup
- 1/2 teaspoon taco seasoning
- 1/2 cup grated yellow cheddar (optional)
- 1 cup finely chopped lettuce

for the avocado sauce
- 1 large mature avocado
- 3 tablespoons lime or lemon juice
- 2 tablespoons yogurt
- a little salt and a little sugar

1. Place the chicken pieces in a large bowl, season with salt and pepper and pour over half the lemon juice and half the olive oil. Sprinkle with half the oregano. Place the tomato and pepper pieces in another bowl, and pour over the remaining juice, oil and oregano. Cover and place both bowls in the refrigerator, to marinate for several hours or overnight.

2. Prepare the tortilla dough and roll out on a floured surface, using a rolling pin. Cut out large butterflies with a 10-cm (5-in) pastry cutter. Cook them in a skillet until bubbles form on the surface. Roll them up and store in the freezer. Just before serving, fry the tortillas in a little corn oil, or heat them in a toaster.

3. Heat the oil for the sauce in a large deep skillet, and sauté the onion and garlic. Drain the chicken from the marinade, and sauté it for 8-10 minutes, until all the pieces of meat are well cooked. Add all the remaining ingredients except the grated cheese and lettuce. Let the chicken simmer in the sauce for another 10 minutes.

4. Prepare the avocado sauce by mixing all the ingredients together, and spread it over the tortillas. Place 2 tablespoons of chopped lettuce onto each tortilla. Drain the pieces of chicken and divide them between the tortillas, together with spoonfuls of the tomato and pepper mixture. Sprinkle the tostadas with the grated cheddar and grill for 10 minutes, until the cheese melts. Serve the tostadas warm or cold, they are equally delicious.

Chicken and pepper pastry roll

Yields 2 rolls (16 portions)
Preparation time 24 hours
Baking time for the chicken 20 minutes
(190°C/375°F), for the rolls 50 minutes
(160°C/325°F)
<u>Suitable for freezing</u>
Degree of difficulty ☺☺☺

- 800g (2lbs) chicken breast fillet
- salt and freshly ground pepper
- 1/3 cup lemon juice
- 1/3 cup olive oil
- 1 teaspoon crumbled dried thyme
- 2 bay leaves
- 2 jars (800g) red roasted peppers
- 400g (14oz) brie
- 500g (1lb) puff pastry, in 2 sheets
- 1 egg yolk for coating
- a little sesame

1. Split the chicken breasts in half and flatten; wrap them in plastic wrap and beat with a meat hammer. Arrange them in a row in a fire-resistant dish, season, and pour over the juice and oil. Sprinkle with the thyme and top with the bay leaves. Cover and refrigerate for 24 hours.

2. Drain the peppers well, cut them in half and place on absorbent paper, to absorb all the oil. Bake the chicken together with the marinade at 190°C (375°C) for 20 minutes. Drain the pieces of chicken and remove to a plate to cool. Cut them in half lengthways. Cut the cheese into long strips.

3. Spread out a large piece of aluminum foil, cover with cling film and lay one sheet of pastry on top. Place 1/4 of the chicken pieces in the center, in pairs to form a rod. Cover with slices of pepper and cheese, another 1/4 of the chicken pieces and red pepper slices on top. Use the cling film to roll up the pastry. Prepare the second roll in the same way. At this stage, cover the rolls with aluminum foil and store in the freezer.

4. Remove from the freezer and defrost. Remove the cling film and spread a little egg yolk on the pastry surface. Sprinkle with a little sesame. Bake at 200°C (400°F) for 15 minutes. Reduce the temperature to 160°C (325°F) and bake for another 35 minutes. Remove from the oven and stand for 10 minutes before cutting. Serve in slices.

Pepperoni Farfalle

Chicken Tartlets

Preparation time 15 minutes
Cooking time 15 minutes
Degree of difficulty ☺

- 500g (1lb) colored farfalle pasta
- 1/4 cup olive oil
- 1 small onion, finely chopped
- 1 orange & 1 red pepper, sliced
- 300g (12oz) Italian pepperoni salami, sliced
- 3 tablespoons ketchup
- 1 tablespoon balsamic vinegar
- 1 tablespoon finely chopped fresh basil or 1 teaspoon Italian herbs

1. Heat the oil in a large skillet and sauté the onion and peppers for 5 minutes, until soft. Add the pepperoni, ketchup, vinegar and basil. Stir for a few minutes over the heat.
2. Boil the pasta in salted water with 2 tablespoons oil. Drain and remove to a large bowl. Pour over the sauce and serve immediately in small bowls for the children. If you like, sprinkle the pasta with grated feta cheese.

Yields 12 tartlets
Preparation time 40 minutes
Cooking time 40 minutes
Degree of difficulty ☺☺

- 1 recipe pâte brisée dough (recipe on page 175)

for the filling
- 600g (16oz) chicken breast, no skin or bones, chopped
- 2 cups vegetable stock
- 3 tablespoons olive oil
- 2 cloves garlic, crushed
- 1 small onion, grated
- 1 can sliced mushrooms, drained
- 1 teaspoon taco seasoning
- 3 tablespoons chili sauce
- 1/2 cup grated white hard cheese
- 6 jarred red peppers, to decorate

1. Divide the dough into 12 small balls. Roll out each one into a round sheet and use them to line a well-greased 8-cm (3-in) tartlet pan with a removable bottom. Line 12 small pie pans in the same way. Bake the tartlets for 15 minutes at 180°C (360°F). Remove from the oven and when cool remove the pie crusts from the pans.
2. Boil the chicken in the broth for 30 minutes, until very soft. Heat the oil in a saucepan and sauté the garlic and onion. Add the chicken pieces and mushrooms and stir for a few minutes over high heat. Add and mix in the seasoning, sauce, salt and a little pepper; cover and simmer for 3 minutes.
3. Fill the pie crusts with the chicken mixture and sprinkle with the grated cheese. Before serving, bake at 180°C (360°F) for 5-7 minutes, until the cheese melts.
4. Split the peppers in half and cut two butterflies out of each half, using a 5-cm (1.5-in) pastry cutter. Garnish the tartlets with the butterflies and serve warm.

Butterfly Cookies

Yields 20-24 cookies
Preparation time 30 minutes
Baking time 10 minutes (180°C/360°F)
Degree of difficulty ☺☺

for the sugar cookie dough
- 3 cups all-purpose flour
- 1/8 teaspoon salt
- 1 teaspoon baking powder
- 1 cup unsalted soft butter

- 1 cup sugar
- 1 large egg
- 2 teaspoons vanilla essence or zest of 1 lemon or 1 orange

for decorating
- 1 egg white, lightly beaten
- hundreds and thousands

1. Sift the flour with the salt and baking powder. Cream the butter and sugar in the mixer at medium speed, until white and fluffy. Add the egg and vanilla or zest and beat to incorporate in the mixture. Add the solid ingredients and beat at low speed, until you obtain soft dough that doesn't stick to the bowl or your hands.

2. Cut pieces off the dough and use a small rolling pin to roll out 5-mm (0.2-in) thick sheets. Use the special pastry cutters to cut out small and large butterflies. Transfer the shapes to an ungreased baking pan and bake for 10 minutes at 180°C (360°F). While hot, remove the cookies from the pan using a metal spatula. Transfer to a rack and let cool completely before decorating.

3. Coat the cookie surface with a little egg white, using a brush, and sprinkle with hundreds and thousands. Leave uncovered for a few hours, so that the egg white dries and the decorations stick to the cookies.

Pink Smoothies

Yields 8 smoothies
Preparation time 15 minutes
Cookingfor children

- 3 cups strawberries, washed and sliced
- 1/2 cup sugar (optional)

- 4 ice cubes
- 2 cups yogurt
- 1 teaspoon vanilla essence
- strawberry sorbet

1. Beat the strawberries with the sugar and ice cubes in the blender, until puréed. If the strawberries are too sweet, use less sugar or none at all. Add the yogurt and vanilla essence and beat to a smooth mixture. Divide the smoothie into glasses and serve, if you like, with scoops of strawberry sorbet. Serve immediately.

Strawberry Sorbet – fruit sorbet

Yields 12 icepops or portions
Preparation time 10 minutes
Cooking for children

- 4 cups frozen fruit pieces
- 3 egg whites or 2 cups yogurt
- 3 tablespoons lemon juice
- 1/2 cup sugar

1. Clean the fruit (peaches, pears, apricots or strawberries) and dice them. Arrange a layer of fruit in a metal box. Cover and freeze for 24 hours, or until solid.

2. Purée the frozen fruit in the mixer (this will be a noisy process). Do not defrost. Add the egg whites, juice and sugar. Alternatively, add the yogurt, if used. Keep beating until you obtain a thick, frozen meringue. Stop, clean the sides of the bowl with a spatula and continue beating, until the meringue softens and climbs up the sides of the bowl. Serve immediately in glasses with fresh fruit and whipped cream or pour into a metal box and store in the freezer. Once cold, you can take out scoops of the sorbet.

3. Alternatively, prepare icepops by dividing the sorbet into 12 round deep icepop molds and attaching the special sticks, so that the kids can hold them when frozen. You can make two-tone icepops by using half peach and half strawberry sorbet in the molds.

Jumbo Butterfly muffins

Yields 12 jumbo muffins
Preparation time 30 minutes
Baking time 40-45 minutes (180°C/360°F)
Suitable for freezing
Degree of difficulty ☺

for the egg whites cake mix
- 3½ cups self-raising flour
- 1²/3 cups sugar
- 2 teaspoons baking powder

- 1 cup (2 sticks) soft butter
- 6 egg whites
- 2/3 cup milk
- 2 teaspoons vanilla essence

for decorating
- 1/2 recipe soft white icing (recipe on page 179)
- pink shiny sugar
- a few long marshmallows

1. Beat all the cake ingredients together in the mixer for 4 minutes, until soft. Line two jumbo muffin trays with white or pink paper cases and pour the mixture into them, to fill around 2/3 of each.

2. Bake the muffins at 180°C (360°F) for 40-45 minutes, or until a skewer comes out clean. Remove the muffins from the oven and let cool. At this stage they can be stored in the freezer, in airtight food bags.

3. Use a piping bag with a #1D nozzle to design the butterfly's wings with icing. Sprinkle with pink shiny sugar. Place two long marshmallows in the center, for the butterfly's body. Make the antennae with thin red wire. Decorate the muffins on the day you plan to serve them. Store at room temperature.

Don't I get a fairy hat?

Two sweet sisters, Anna and Myrsini

This candy floss is delicious!

Macaroni 'n' Cheese

Yields 12 portions
Preparation time 20 minutes
Baking time 20 minutes (200°C/400°F)
Degree of difficulty ☺

- 1/3 cup butter
- 2 tablespoons all-purpose flour
- 2½ cups milk
- 2 cups grated mozzarella for pizza
- 1/2 cup grated hard yellow cheese
- 500g (1lb) cavatapi pasta

to cover, choose between:
- 1 cup grated stale bread and
  3 tablespoons olive oil or
  6 slices bacon, finely chopped and
  sautéed or
  2 tablespoons finely chopped
  fresh rosemary

1. Melt the butter in a large deep saucepan. Sauté the flour in it. Pour all the milk into the saucepan at once. Simmer, stirring constantly, until the cream starts to set.

2. Remove from the heat, add half the cheeses, and stir until melted. Boil the pasta in plenty of salted water with 2 tablespoons oil. Drain and pour into a well-buttered oven dish.

3. Pour over the sauce and sprinkle with the remaining cheeses. Cover with either stale breadcrumbs sautéed in oil, or crispy bacon, or rosemary. Children love the bacon, while adults prefer the delicate aroma of rosemary.

4. Bake the macaroni'n'cheese at 200°C (400°F) for 15-20 minutes, or until the surface turns golden brown. Serve warm, in individual bowls.

Conney Island Hot Dogs

Yields 12 hot dogs
Preparation time 20 minutes
Degree of difficulty ☺

- 12 Frankfurters
- 12 long buns (recipe on page 155)
- salt and pepper
- mustard for serving

1. Make lengthways incisions in the Frankfurters with a knife, so that they don't burst while boiling. Boil in salted water. Remove to a platter using a fork. At this stage, the sausages can be refrigerated, covered, until serving time. Prepare the relish you want to use.
2. Slice the buns open lengthways, and place a boiled Frankfurter and 1-2 tablespoons relish inside. Children prefer simple tastes, such as red pepper relish or easy relish. Garnish with a little mustard and serve the hot dogs warm.
3. For greater ease, prepare the plate of buns and hot dogs, without the sauces, on the day before, and store covered in the refrigerator. Just before serving, place two small pieces of margarine or butter on each hot dog and heat for 5 minutes at 200°C (400°F).

Easy Relish

- 2 red peppers, finely chopped
- 2 tomatoes, finely chopped
- 10 basil leaves, finely chopped
- 1 small onion, finely chopped
- 1 clove garlic, finely chopped
- 2-3 tablespoons ketchup
- a little salt

1. Mix all the above ingredients together. Keep the relish refrigerated for up to 2 days.

American dream Salad

Yields 12 portions
Preparation time 15 minutes
Degree of difficulty ☺

- 12 slices sandwich bread
- 6 slices bacon, chopped
- 1/2 teaspoon Italian herbs
- 400g (14oz) canned corn
- 16 cherry tomatoes, sliced in half
- 3 red peppers, thinly sliced
- 3 green onions, finely chopped
- 6 pickled gherkins, thinly sliced
- a little salt

for the honey-mustard dressing
- 1/3 cup extra-virgin olive oil
- 3 tablespoons vinegar
- 2 teaspoons mustard
- 2 tablespoons honey

1. Cut stars out of each slice of bread using a 7-cm (3-in) pastry cutter. Sauté the bacon in a small skillet, until crisp. Remove to a plate. Fry the bread stars in the bacon fat. Sprinkle with the herbs inside the skillet and drizzle with a tablespoon of oil. Toast the stars well on either side and remove to the same plate as the bacon. You can cut the stars out of baked tortillas and then fry them in a little oil.
2. Drain the corn and pour into a large bowl. Add and mix in the remaining ingredients, then add the sautéed mixture. It is a good idea to sauté the bacon and bread on the party day, just before serving the salad.
3. Place all the dressing ingredients in a jar and shake to mix together. Drizzle the salad with the dressing, just before serving.

T-Bone Steak

For a crowd
Preparation time 15 minutes
Cooking time 20-25 minutes
Degree of difficulty ☺

- 6 thick T-bone steaks
- 6 tablespoons Worcestershire sauce
- 6 teaspoons honey
- 6 tablespoons lemon juice
- 6 tablespoons whisky

for the aromatic butter
- 1/2 cup soft unsalted butter
- 2 cloves garlic, crushed
- 1/4 teaspoon salt
- 1/2 teaspoon pepper
- 1 teaspoon dried parsley

for garnishing
- a few fresh, tender corn cobs
- a few large potatoes
- BBQ sauce and mustard

1. Mix the Worcestershire sauce with the honey, lemon juice, whisky, salt and pepper. Coat the steaks with the mixture and store for 20 minutes in the refrigerator. Drain off the marinade and place the steaks on a double grill. Barbecue for 8-10 minutes on each side (depending on how well-done you like them), basting with the marinade every now and again. Serve the T-bone steaks on a wooden plate or special board, accompanied with baked potatoes and boiled or barbecued corn. If you like, chop the meat up and serve on a platter, for all the guests.

2. Beat the butter with the garlic, salt, pepper and parsley. Refrigerate until slightly set. The butter must be soft, so that you can use a piping bag to make butter rosettes on each steak and potato, and on the corn, if you like. Cook as many potatoes and corn cobs as the children at the party. Serve BBQ sauce, finely chopped onion and mustard in small bowls, to accompany the steaks.

Baked potatoes

For a crowd
Preparation time 15 minutes
Cooking time 1 hour 30 minutes
Degree of difficulty ☺

- 6 medium potatoes, uniform in shape
- 1/2 cup finely chopped green onions
- 1/4 cup finely chopped parsley or dill or mint
- 2 cups sour cream
- 1/4 cup finely chopped red pepper
- salt and freshly ground black pepper

1. Wash the potatoes and dry them well. Wrap each one in aluminum foil and place then in the hot ashes below the lit coals, or bake in the oven at 200°C (400°F). Bake for about 1 hour 30 minutes, until soft.

2. Mix the onions and parsley in a small bowl. For the potatoes to open up like flowers, make deep crisscross incisions on the top, and press on either side off the bottom with your fingers. Sprinkle with salt and freshly ground pepper. Serve with sour cream or a little aromatic butter, herbs and green onion.

Ice cream cakes

Yields 12 cakes
Preparation time 25 minutes
Baking time 40-45 minutes
(175°C/350°F)
Degree of difficulty ☺

- 1 recipe chocolate cake
- 12 chocolate ice cream cones
- 1 recipe white icing
- colored or chocolate sprinkles

1. Prepare ice cream cakes, an idea that children will absolutely love. Prepare one recipe chocolate cake. Arrange the ice cream cones on an unbuttered baking pan. Pour in the cake mix, filling about 2/3 of each cone. Bake in the oven at 175°C (350°F) for 40-45 minutes, or until a skewer comes out clean.

2. Garnish the cakes with white icing and cover with colored or chocolate sprinkles. Will keep for several days, covered, at room temperature. You can also serve the cone cakes with scoops of ice cream instead of icing.

3. Alternatively, make white ice cream cones with vanilla cake or strawberry cake, and serve with strawberry icing.

Nachos Pazzos

For a crowd
Preparation time 30 minutes
Degree of difficulty ☺☺

- 20 cooked 10-cm (4-in) tortillas or 500g (1lb) store-bought nachos
- 1/2 cup vegetable oil
- 1 cup red pepper relish or easy relish
- 2 cups chili ground meat sauce (recipe follows)
- 250g (8oz) grated yellow cheddar, melted, or store-bought melted cheese sauce for nachos
- 2 tablespoons fresh coriander or finely chopped parsley
- 1 cup guacamole and sour cream

1. To make your own nachos, stack the tortillas one on top of the other and cut them in half using a sharp knife. Cut each half into 3 triangular slices, to make 6 nachos out of each tortilla. Heat the oil in a small, deep saucepan. Fry the tortilla slices, overturning at least once, until golden brown. Remove with a slotted spoon and drain on absorbent paper.

2. Preheat the oven to 200°C (400°F). Arrange the nachos in one or more round oven dishes, and spread over the relish and chili. Sprinkle with the cheddar and bake for 10 minutes, until the cheese melts, or pour over the melted cheese sauce. Sprinkle with the coriander and serve immediately with guacamole and sour cream.

Chili Ground Meat Sauce ("Sloppy Joe" Burgers)

Yields 4 cups
Preparation time 20 minutes
Cooking time 1 hour
Degree of difficulty ☺

- 1/3 cup olive oil
- 1kg (2lbs) ground meat (1/2 beef and 1/2 pork)
- 2 cloves garlic, crushed
- 1 medium onion, grated
- 1/2 cup finely chopped green pepper
- 1/4 teaspoon cumin, 1 teaspoon paprika,
- 1 teaspoon chili powder, 1 teaspoon oregano, 1 teaspoon salt, 1/2 teaspoon coriander, 1/2 teaspoon cinnamon, 1/4 teaspoon clove powder
- 800g (2lbs) canned tomatoes
- 1/2 cup orange juice
- 2 tablespoons tomato paste
- 1/4 cup finely chopped parsley or coriander
- 200g (7oz) canned red kidney beans

1. Heat the oil in a large deep skillet and sauté the ground meat for 8 minutes, stirring to divide it into small pieces. Reduce the heat, add and mix in the garlic and onion. Add all the remaining ingredients except the beans, and bring to the boil.

2. Reduce the heat, cover and simmer for 1 hour, stirring occasionally. Add and mix in the beans during the last 15 minutes.

3. You can also serve the ground meat chili sauce in bowls, sprinkled with grated cheddar cheese. Use the chili as a filling for a delicious original pasta soufflé, to fill cannelloni or serve with nachos. Alternatively, prepare "Sloppy Joe" hamburgers with the chili ground meat sauce; children love them.

Guacamole Avocado Dip

Yields 2 cups
Preparation time 20 minutes

- 4 large ripe avocados
- 1/4 cup freshly squeezed lime or lemon juice
- 6 green onions, finely chopped
- 5 drops Tabasco sauce
- 1/4 cup finely chopped coriander or parsley
- 2 medium tomatoes, skinned and diced
- 1/2 cup finely chopped red and green pepper
- salt and white pepper

1. A very nutritious and delicious dip that kids will love. For the guacamole you serve to the adults, add as much Tabasco sauce and green onion as you like. For the kids, avoid both.

2. Peel the avocados and pour over the lemon juice immediately. Chop up two of the avocados with a knife, and place the pieces in a bowl. Mash the other two avocados with a fork or pulp them in the blender. Transfer the avocado purée to the bowl with the avocado pieces and add the green onions, Tabasco, coriander, tomato cubes and finely chopped pepper. Serve the dip with nachos or fresh vegetable sticks, such as cucumber, celery, and carrot cut in even, thin sticks.

Red pepper relish

For everyone at the party
Preparation time 20 minutes
Cooking time 1 hour 45 minutes
Time prior to serving 1 week
Degree of difficulty ☺

- 1kg (2lbs) red peppers, in julienne pieces
- 1 teaspoon black peppercorns
- 2 teaspoons mustard seeds
- 2 onions, thinly sliced
- 4 cloves garlic, finely chopped
- 1½ cups fine quality wine vinegar
- 2 hard cooking apples, peeled and grated
- 1 teaspoon grated fresh ginger
- 1 cup brown sugar

1. Wrap the peppercorns and mustard seeds in veiling and place them in a large saucepan, together with the peppers, onions, garlic, vinegar, grated apple and ginger. Simmer for 30 minutes, until the peppers soften.

2. Add the sugar and mix until dissolved. Simmer, stirring occasionally, for 1 hour 15 minutes, or until the relish sets well. Remove the veiling with the pepper and mustard seeds. Pour the mixture into sterilized jars. Cover the jars and let the relish stand for 1-2 weeks before using.

3. Will keep for up to 1 year in a cool, shady place. Once opened, keep the jars refrigerated. Do not forget to label the jars, indicating the content and production date.

Quesadillas with ground meat or avocado

Yields 16 pieces
Preparation time 15 minutes
Baking time 10 minutes (200°C/400°F)
Degree of difficulty ☺

- 16 tortillas
- 2 cups (500g - 1lb) guacamole sauce
  (recipe on page 103) or
  2 cups chili sauce
  (recipe on page 103)
- 2 cups easy relish (recipe on page 98)
- 2 cups grated cheddar or
  mozzarella cheese

1. Prepare tortilla quesadillas by filling them with the rest of the ingredients. Use 4 tortillas at a time, to make one quesadilla; i.e. you should make a total of 4 tortilla clusters.

2. Place 4 tortillas next to one another on a tray covered with non-stick oven paper. Cover with a little grated cheese, a little relish, a little ground meat or guacamole, and grated cheese on top. Cover the filling with another tortilla and repeat the layers. End with a tortilla.

3. Bake the quesadillas at 200°C (400°F) for 10 minutes, just enough for the cheese to melt. Remove from the oven and cut into quarters using a sharp knife. This will give you 16 pieces of stuffed tortilla. Stick a cocktail flag into each piece, and serve on a platter. Serve with guacamole sauce if not used in the filling.

Cheerleaders' Bâtons

Yields 12 mini pastries
Preparation time 10 minutes + 30
minutes refrigeration
Baking time 30 minutes (210°C/415°F)
Degree of difficulty ☺

- 3 tablespoons sugar
- 1 teaspoon cinnamon
- 1 teaspoon orange zest
- 250g (8oz) pastry (1 sheet)
- 1 egg yolk beaten with
  1 teaspoon water
- 2 tablespoons apricot jam
- 1 cup maraschino cherry halves,
  well drained

1. Mix the sugar, cinnamon and orange zest. Coat half the pastry sheet with egg yolk and sprinkle with the cinnamon-and-sugar. Then coat with the apricot jam, heated and softened, and sprinkle with cherry halves.

2. Fold over the other half of the pastry sheet and press down. Cut 2-cm (1/8-in) strips off the oblong pastry sandwich. Twist the pastry strips with your hands, and arrange them on an oven dish lined with non-stick paper. Refrigerate for 30 minutes.

3. Bake the pastries on the oven's top shelf at 210°C (415°F) for 15 minutes, until they rise. Reduce the temperature to 150°C (300°F), and continue baking for another 15 minutes. Remove the pastries from the oven and let cool inside the dish. Serve to the kids, with glasses of fresh lemonade.

Oven-baked potatoes

Yields 8 portions
Preparation time 20 minutes
Baking time 40 minutes (200°C/400°F)
Degree of difficulty ☺

- 2kg (4lbs) potatoes
- 1 teaspoon salt
- 1 tablespoon dry herb mix
  (oregano, thyme, basil, rosemary)
- 3-4 tablespoons olive oil

1. On the day before the party, peel and chop the potatoes into long thin pieces. If you like, you can leave the skin on, if it is clean and smooth. Keep the potatoes in a bowl in the refrigerator, covered with water.

2. Drain the potatoes and dry on absorbent paper. Arrange in an oven dish lined with greaseproof paper. Sprinkle with the salt and herbs and drizzle with the oil. Bake at 200°C (400°F) for 35-40 minutes, or until golden and crispy. Serve in paper cones with 1 tablespoon mayonnaise or ketchup.

Dream Strawberry Roll

Yields 10 portions
Preparation time 30 minutes
Baking time 12 minutes (200°C/400°F)

for the sponge cake
- 3 large eggs
- 1/2 cup sugar
- 3/4 cup self-raising flour
- 2 tablespoons warm water
- icing sugar for sprinkling

for the filling
- 1½ cups cream
- 4 tablespoons icing sugar
- a little vanilla powder
- 1/2 cup strawberry jam
- 250g (8oz) fresh strawberries

1. Prepare the sponge cake. Butter a baking pan or jelly roll pan (dimensions 30x26 cm/ 12x10 in) and line with non-stick oven paper.
2. Beat the eggs and sugar in the mixer, until fluffy and double in volume, about 15 minutes. Sift the flour into the mixer bowl and beat at very low speed for a few seconds, or mix in softly with a wooden spoon, until incorporated in the beaten eggs. Add the warm water a little at a time, mixing it gently, and taking care not to deflate the eggs.
3. Pour the mixture into the pan and smooth down the surface with a metal spatula. Bake in a pre-heated oven at 200°C (400°F) for 10-12 minutes. Remove from the oven and overturn onto a cloth covered with greaseproof paper and sprinkled with icing sugar. Detach the greaseproof paper carefully from the top of the sponge cake. Roll up the cake gently while it is still hot, with the cloth and new paper. This way it won't break when you fill it. Stand for 20-30 minutes, until completely cold.
4. Wash the strawberries thoroughly and slice them thinly. Keep a few slices for garnishing. Beat the cream with the icing sugar and vanilla, until thick. Unroll the sponge cake, coat with the heated, soft jam, and cover with 2/3 of the whipped cream and the strawberry slices. Roll up again carefully and transfer the dessert to a serving platter. Garnish with the remaining whipped cream and strawberries. Keep the roll uncovered in the refrigerator. Sprinkle with a little icing sugar before serving. Will keep for 2 days in the refrigerator.

Stars 'n' spangles gâteau

Yields 12 portions
Preparation time 30 minutes
Baking time 35 minutes (180°C/360°F)
<u>Suitable for freezing (final stage)</u>
Degree of difficulty ☺☺

for the blue sponge cake
- 5 large eggs
- 1¼ cups sugar
- 1¼ cups self-raising flour
- 2½ teaspoons vanilla powder
- a few drops blue food coloring
- 2 tablespoons water
- 3 tablespoons melted butter
- 1 deep round baking pan, 24-cm (9-in)

for the filling
- 3 cups whipping cream
- 1/3 cup icing sugar
- 2 teaspoons vanilla powder
- 400g (14oz) fresh strawberries,
  washed and sliced

for the icing
- 2 packets (450g/ 15oz each)
  store-bought icing or
  1 recipe soft white icing
  (recipe on page 179)
- blue and red sugared star-shaped sprinkles

1. Beat the eggs and sugar in the mixer at medium speed, until thick and double in volume, about 15 minutes. Stop beating and sift in the flour, a little at a time, folding into the mixture gently, so as not to deflate the egg mixture. Finally, add the food coloring, diluted in the water, and the melted butter; beat for a few seconds at very low speed, to obtain a smooth mixture.

2. Butter the baking pan and line the bottom with non-stick paper, also buttered; then pour in the sponge cake mix. Bake the cake at 180°C (360°F) for 35-40 minutes, or until a skewer comes out clean.

3. Remove the cake from the oven, overturn once, remove the paper, and overturn again onto a rack, covered with non-stick paper, so that the risen side faces upwards. Leave to cool.

4. Beat the cream, sugar and vanilla in the mixer until thick. If the mixture is too runny, add 1/2 teaspoon gelatin, diluted in 2 tablespoons water and heated, or 1 sachet cream thickener.

5. Divide the sponge cake into three layers, and place one on a serving platter. Cover the cake with a layer of whipped cream and arrange half the strawberry slices on top. Cover with another layer of cream and the second cake layer. Repeat the layers and cover with the last cake layer. Cover the whole cake with white icing and sprinkle over the sugared stars. Refrigerate the gâteau for 2-3 hours, until set.

Yields 20 pieces
Preparation time 20 minutes
Baking time 1 hour (190°C/375°F)
Degree of difficulty ☺☺

for the brownies
- 1½ cups cake flour, not self-raising
- 2 teaspoons baking powder
- 1/2 cup unsweetened cocoa
- 1/4 teaspoon each nutmeg,
  clove, cinnamon powder
- 1/2 cup margarine
- 2 cups brown sugar
- 1/2 cup sunflower oil
- 1 teaspoon vanilla essence
- 1/2 cup evaporated milk
- 3 large eggs

- 3 cups grated zucchini
  (around 500g/ 1lb)
- 100g (4oz) grated chocolate or
  chocolate chips

for the soft green icing
- 2/3 cup white vegetable shortening
- 1/2 cup cream cheese, softened
- 3 cups icing sugar
- 2-3 tablespoons milk
- 1 teaspoon bitter almond or
  peppermint essence
- a few drops green food coloring

1. Mix the flour with the baking powder, cocoa and spices in a large bowl. Beat the margarine with the sugar, oil and vanilla in the mixer at high speed, until the mixture is soft and fluffy, around 3-5 minutes. Add the milk and the eggs and beat for 2 minutes at high speed. Pour the solids mixture and the zucchini into the mixer bowl and fold in gently.

2. Coat a 23x33 cm (9x12 in) rectangular baking pan with a little margarine and line the bottom and sides with non-stick paper. Coat again with a little margarine. Pour the cake mix into the mold and smooth down the surface with a spatula. Sprinkle here and there with the grated chocolate. Bake the cake at 190°C (375°F) for 50 minutes to 1 hour, or until a skewer comes out dry. Remove from the oven and let cool in the baking pan.

3. Prepare the icing. Cream the butter and cream cheese in the mixer at low speed, until fluffy. Add the sugar and beat at medium speed, to incorporate. Add as much milk as necessary to give the icing the right texture. Add the essence and a few drops green food coloring. Spread the icing over the cake. Use a knife to divide the cake into pieces, without cutting all the way through. Decorate with marzipan vegetables. Will keep for 2 days in the refrigerator.

Savory Carrot Pie and Zucchini Tartlets

Yields 16 portions
Preparation time 1 hour
Baking time 30 minutes (200°C/400°F)
Degree of difficulty ☺☺

for the pie crust
- 2 cups plain flour
- 1/2 cup milk
- 1/4 cup oil
- 1/4 cup margarine
- 1 teaspoon salt
- 1 oven-proof pie pan, 30-cm (12-in)

for the filling
- 1kg (2lbs) carrots
- 1/3 cup unsalted butter
- 1/2 cup grated onion
- 1/3 cup chopped green onions
- 1 small clove garlic, crushed
- 1/3 cup finely chopped parsley
- 1/3 cup finely chopped mint
- 2 cups grated hard yellow cheese
- 2 large eggs, lightly beaten
- 4 tablespoons double cream
- a little grated nutmeg

1. Grease the pie pan thoroughly. Place all the pastry ingredients in a large bowl and knead. Roll out a sheet of pastry on a piece of Cabot material sprinkled with a little flour and spread into the pie pan, covering the bottom and sides.
2. Boil the carrots in salted water, until quite soft, drain and reserve 3 whole ones. Mash the rest in the mixer together with the water they boiled in, to make a purée. Cut the reserved carrots into slices, and set aside.
3. Melt the butter in a saucepan and sauté the onions and garlic. Remove from the heat, add and mix in the herbs and the carrot purée. Add the cheese, eggs, cream and nutmeg, and mix gently. Pour the mixture over the pie crust and garnish the surface with the carrot slices, sautéed in 1 tablespoon butter. Bake the pie at 200°C (400°F) for 30 minutes.

Alternatively: Use the same pie pastry to make 12 7-cm (5in) tartlets or 24 mini tartlets, and bake them for 20 minutes at 200°C (400°F), having pricked the surface with a fork. You can also purchase ready-made mini tartlets. Grate 6 zucchini using a coarse grater and blanch briefly. Drain, mix with 1 cup pesto sauce, and fill the tartlets with the mixture. Serve cold with thin slices of Parmesan and cherry tomatoes.

Yields 16 portions
Preparation time several hours
Baking time 1 hour (180°C/360°F)
Degree of difficulty ☺☺☺

- 3 cups self-raising flour
- 2 cups sugar
- a little salt
- 2 ripe bananas, mashed
- 4 eggs
- 1 cup soft butter
- 1/2 cup milk
- 2/3 cup yogurt
- 1 teaspoon vanilla extract
- 1 3D "Beetle" baking pan
- 1 baking rod (optional)

for decorating
- 2kg (4lbs) Regalice sugar paste
- 1/2 cup raspberry jam
- icing sugar for dusting
- green, orange, violet, black and yellow
  food coloring paste
- "love" pastry cutters
- tear-shaped pastry cutters in various sizes

1. Place all the cake ingredients in the mixer bowl and beat for 4 minutes at medium speed. Pour the dough into a well-buttered and floured 3D beetle car mold. Bake the cake in an oven preheated to 180°C (360°F) for 1 hour. Perform the skewer test, pricking the cake in its center and if necessary continue baking for a further 10 minutes, or until the skewer comes out dry.
2. Remove the cake from the oven and let stand for 10 minutes in the mold. Overturn onto a serving platter and let cool. At this stage, you can cut the cake lengthways into two layers and fill it with your favorite filling or with crème pâtissière. Then freeze for several hours, covered. A frozen cake is easier to decorate.
3. Color one packet of Regalice with orange food coloring paste; you will need about 1/2 teaspoon. Knead well with your hands on a surface sprinkled with icing sugar, until the color is uniform. Use two long pieces of string to measure the car from one side to the other and from the front to the rear bumper. Use a rolling pin to roll out the orange Regalice into an oblong sheet, with dimensions equal to the two lengths of string.
4. Heat a little raspberry jam, pass it through a sieve until transparent, and use it to coat the car-shaped cake. Wrap the sheet of Regalice carefully around a thin wooden rod, sprinkled with icing sugar, and transfer it onto the car. Smooth the sugar paste carefully over the entire surface. Use a sharp knife to cut off bits of the icing on either side to make the windows. Make paper patterns using the cake mold as a guide. Cut out the car's windscreen and rear window. Remove the orange icing.
5. Use the patterns to cut 4 side windows and two windscreens out of white icing and stick them on using a little raspberry jam. Use the pastry cutters to cut the word LOVE out of the orange icing, and cover the gaps with letters cut out of colored sugar paste, dyed with food coloring. Also cut out flower petals with a tear-shaped pastry cutter on the car's hood, and make daisies with different colored icing.
6. Cut out white wheels and stick them onto the relevant places with a little water, over the orange icing. Make two thick laces with your hands and stick them on for the front and rear bumper, using a little water; stick on small white or yellow balls for the head- and tail-lights. Use your imagination to create a fantastic '70s-style birthday cake. Have Fun!

Yields 20 portions
Preparation time 1 hour + 2 hours to rise
Suitable for freezing
Baking time 50 minutes (180°C/360°F)

- 1 recipe brioche dough
  (recipe on page 113)
- 1 guitar-shaped baking mold
- 1 recipe guacamole dip
  (recipe on page 103)
- 1 cup soft cheese cream or mayonnaise
- 1 cup olive paste
- 20 slices Milan salami
- 10 slices Mortadella
- carrot and cucumber sticks
- 3 red peppers, cut in triangular pieces

1. Prepare the bread dough and press it into a well-buttered guitar mold, to cover the entire bottom. Cover with cling film and let the dough rise for 30 minutes, or until it reaches the rim of the mold. Bake the bread at 180°C (360°F) for 45-50 minutes, or until the surface is golden. Remove from the oven and let stand for 10 minutes inside the mold. Overturn onto a rack and let cool. At this stage, the bread can be covered and stored in the freezer for up to 1 month.
2. To serve, place the bread in a large pretty serving dish. Use a sharp knife to cut a hole in the center of the guitar. Line the opening with a little cling film and fill with the guacamole or any other dip you prefer. If you like, coat the bread with soft cream cheese or mayonnaise, and use a piping bag to make the guitar strings with black olive paste. Garnish with cold cooked meats and serve with vegetable sticks.

Yields 20 portions
Preparation time 35 minutes
Baking time 1 hour (180°C/360°F)
Suitable for freezing (final stage)
Degree of difficulty ☺☺

for the green cake
- 2 boxes store-bought white cake mix
- 200g (7oz) yogurt
- 6 egg whites
- 1²/3 cups milk
- 2/3 cup corn oil
- a few drops green food coloring
- 1 round deep baking pan (28cm/ 11in)

for the filling and decoration
- 1 kg whipping cream
- 1/2 cup icing sugar
- 1 sachet instant vanilla pudding
- green food coloring
- 500g (1lb) fresh strawberries, washed and chopped
- 1 football player candle
- 12 sugar footballs

1. Coat the round baking pan with butter and sprinkle it with flour. Beat all the cake ingredients together in the mixer bowl, for 3 minutes at high speed. Pour the cake mix into the baking pan and bake at 180°C (360°F) for 55-60 minutes.
2. Remove from the oven, overturn onto a rack and let cool. Cut the cake into three layers using a sharp knife. Beat the cream with the icing sugar and instant pudding until set. Cover the cake layers with half the whipped cream and the strawberry pieces. Assemble the cake.
3. Color the remaining cream with green food coloring and use it to cover the cake. Spread the cream with a metal spatula. Place any leftover cream in a piping bag and make pretty balls all around the top of the cake. Refrigerate the cake for at least 4 hours. Decorate the sides of the cake with the sugar footballs and place the football player candle in the center. Sprinkle the cake surface with green caster sugar. Depending on the child's age and favorite football team, decorate the cake with the relevant number of red, green, yellow, blue or white candles.

Club Sandwich

Coleslaw

Yields 16 mini sandwiches
Preparation time 30 minutes
<u>Cooking for kids</u>

- 4 slices tomato
- 8 small tender lettuce leaves
- 4 slices ham or smoked turkey or 200g (7oz) boiled chicken
- 4 square slices soft yellow cheese
- salt, pepper
- 200g (7oz) bacon
- 12 slices sandwich bread
- 1 cup mayonnaise

1. Grill the bacon. Toast the bread slices and spread them with mayonnaise. Place the cheese and smoked turkey or chicken onto four slices of bread. Cover with four more slices of bread, also spread with mayonnaise, and cover with the bacon, lettuce and tomato. Cover with the last four slices of bread.
2. Stick toothpicks into the four sandwich corners, and then cut the sandwiches with a sharp knife, to make 16 mini snacks. Serve with crisps and coleslaw.

Yields 2 cups salad
Preparation time 25 minutes + 1 hour refrigeration
Degree of difficulty ☺

- 1 small cabbage, grated (250g/ 8oz)
- 1/4 cup vinegar
- 4 carrots, grated
- 1 small onion, grated
- 1 cup mayonnaise
- 1/3 cup strained yogurt
- 1 teaspoon horseradish
- 1 teaspoon mustard
- salt and pepper

1. Place the cabbage and vinegar in a bowl and let stand in the refrigerator for at least 24 hours. On the day you plan to serve the salad, drain the cabbage and mix it with carrot and onion.
2. In a small bowl, mix the mayonnaise with the yogurt, horseradish, mustard, salt and pepper. Pour the sauce onto the vegetables and mix in gently. Cover the bowl with cling film and stand in the refrigerator for 1 hour, before serving.

Mini Bagels

Yields 20 mini bagels
Preparation time 2 hours
Baking time 25 minutes (200°C/400°F)
Degree of difficulty ☺☺

- 1¼ cups warm milk (40°C/75°F)
- 1 teaspoon salt
- 3 tablespoons sugar
- 1/3 cup melted butter
- 1 tablespoon dry yeast
- 1 egg, separated
- 4 cups all-purpose flour
- 2 tablespoons poppy seeds

1. Boil the milk in a small saucepan. Remove from the heat and add the salt, sugar and butter. Stir until the butter melts and the sugar dissolves. Pour the mixture into the mixer bowl, and when it reaches 40°C (75°F), add and mix in the yeast. Let it stand until frothy. Add the egg yolk and mix in briskly. Add as much flour as necessary, a little at a time, adding and then kneading with the dough hook for 10 minutes, to obtain elastic dough that doesn't stick to your fingers.

2. Cover and let the dough rise for 1 hour, or until double in volume. Divide into 20 equal pieces. Knead them into small balls and make a hole in the center with your finger, so that they look like donuts. Twist them around your index finger to widen the hole. Place the bagels in a baking pan lined with non-stick paper, cover, and let rise for 10 minutes.

3. Drop the bagels into simmering water and boil them for 15 seconds. Remove with a slotted spoon and arrange on a buttered tray. Beat the egg yolk with 1 teaspoon water, coat the bagels, and then sprinkle them with poppy seeds. Bake at 200°C (400°F) for 25 minutes.

Mini Bagel Sandwiches

Cooking for kids

1. Cut the bagels in two, lengthways, using a sharp knife. Arrange the bottom halves on a tray or platter. Divide the sandwich ingredients into plastic bowls. Pack all the ingredients and assemble the sandwiches at the picnic site, or prepare them at home. The ingredients below are the best for bagel sandwiches. For sweet filling: cream cheese with raspberry jam, peanut butter, and chocolate hazelnut spread. For savory filling: mayonnaise with omelet and finely chopped green onion, mayonnaise and ketchup and various sliced cold meats.

2. Here are some excellent sandwich fillings for older sports fans, i.e. the daddies taking part in the picnic: melted Camembert cheese with currant jelly, cream cheese with finely chopped green onion and smoked salmon, cream cheese with pesto sauce and prosciutto.

Fresh Lemonade

Yields 10 glasses
Degree of difficulty ☺

- 2 cups sugar
- 2 cups water
- 3 cups lemon juice (around 16 lemons)
- 2 cups soda water
- crushed ice

1. In a small saucepan, dissolve the sugar in the water and stir over high heat. Bring the mixture to the boil, then lower the heat and simmer for 5 minutes, to obtain thin syrup. Remove from the heat and place the saucepan in a large bowl of ice cubes, so that the syrup cools quickly.
2. Mix the lemon juice, the syrup, and soda water, and as much crushed ice as you like, and serve the lemonade in a large pitcher. Store covered in the refrigerator. For a larger quantity and sweeter lemonade, add 4 cups orange juice (around 12 oranges).

Shamrock and Football Lollipops

Yields 50 lollipops
Preparation time 30 minutes
Refrigeration time 30 minutes
Cooking for kids

- 400g (16oz) white candy melts
- 200g (8oz) green candy melts
- 200g (8oz) red candy melts
- plastic football and clove lollipop molds
- 2 packets lollipop sticks
- 3 disposable piping bags
- 1 packet special lollipop bags

1. To make the lollipops, you will need plastic chocolate molds and lollipop sticks. Place the green, red and white candy melts in three separate disposable piping bags. Use a pair of scissors to cut the tip off each bag. Melt in a microwave oven for better results. Heat at medium temperature for 1 minute initially. Heat for another minute and proceed, testing each time to see if the candy melts are as fluid as necessary.
2. Pipe red and white mixture into the football molds. Pipe green and white mixture into the shamrock molds Make sure the molds are clean and dry before filling them. When they are full to the rim with the fluid mixture, press a lollipop stick into each mold, and refrigerate for 20 minutes, or until the chocolate sets. Remove from the refrigerator and overturn onto a platter lined with non-stick paper. Tap the mold lightly and the lollipops will drop onto the paper. Store at room temperature, away from direct sunlight and humidity. Store covered in special lollipop bags.

Mini Apple Croissants

Yields 32 mini croissants
Preparation time 20 minutes
Baking time 15 minutes (200°C/400°F)
Degree of difficulty ☺

- 500g (1lb) store-bought or
  homemade croissant dough or
  4 packets refrigerator dough
- 1 egg yolk, beaten with 1 tablespoon water

for the filling
- 2 cups peeled apple pieces
- 4 tablespoons lemon juice
- 1 teaspoon apple pie spice
  (or 1/2 teaspoon cinnamon,
  1/4 teaspoon clove powder and
  1/4 teaspoon nutmeg)
- 4 tablespoons sugar
- 1 cup ground walnuts

1. Prepare the filling. Peel and core the apples, chop them up and place them in a small saucepan, with the lemon juice, cinnamon, clove powder, nutmeg and sugar. Simmer for 5-7 minutes, until the apples are soft and the juices set. Remove from the heat and mix with the ground walnuts.
2. Divide the homemade croissant dough into four sections. Roll out each section into a 15-cm (6-in) circle, and divide into 8 slices. If you are using store-bought dough, it will already be divided into triangles. For mini croissants, each triangle will have to be cut in two.
3. Place a little filling at the base of each triangular piece. Starting from the base, gently wrap each piece into a roll, carefully closing in the filling so that it doesn't run in the oven. Arrange the rolls, with the end facing down, on an unbuttered baking pan, and gently twist the ends to form a crescent. Cover and let the croissants rise until double in volume. Coat with a little egg yolk and bake at 200°C (400°F) for 12-15 minutes. Serve warm. Store in the freezer, in plastic bags, or serve on the same day.

Alternatively: for your picnic, prepare savory mini croissants. Mix 500g (1lb) feta cheese with 2 tablespoons cream and a little pepper; you can also add, for extra taste, 3 tablespoons finely chopped mint or 1/4 cup olive paste. Fill the triangular dough pieces and bake as above.

Sunday, June 6th: Lefteris, Fanis and Phillipos at George's birthday party

Back to school...152 Christmas Surprise...164 Valentine's sweetheart party...188 Invitation to my doll's tea party...206 Good witches and small wizards' Halloween party...222

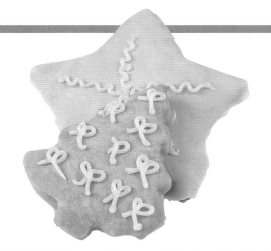

Back to school...

(FOR BOYS 👋 AND GIRLS 👧 AGED 6 AND ABOVE)

The first autumn party can be combined with the beginning of the school year and is a good opportunity for the children to get closer, to meet new school-friends and to create a suitable climate for new friendships. Be innovative; create a homemade invitation in your kitchen. Make autumn leaf cookies out of gingerbread dough with the children, and write the names of each young guest on the cookies with icing. To make the invitations, use a cookie mold to draw a Canadian maple leaf of thin paper in autumn colors. Make as many leaves as the number of guests. Cut the leaves out and write a message on them. Cut the same shape out of cardboard. Stick the invitation written on orange or gold paper onto the cardboard leaf. Make small plastic bags and put each invitation inside together with the cookie with each guest's name on it. Your child can share them out at school; remember that kids love giving invitations and acting like true party hosts.

During the party, the children can be occupied creatively if you provide a space where they can decorate their school exercise books. Spread transparent plastic on the floor in one of the rooms, where there is least danger of damage, and place an old table in the center. Place chairs around it, and give the children exercise books, glue, pens, paper and cardboard, scissors, leaves from the garden, pieces of material, watercolors or anything else they can use safely in the space provided to decorate their books.

Organize the party well by preparing some of the food several days in advance. The apple pie, savory pumpkin tartlets and turkey pie can be stored in the freezer. Prepare the above dishes up to the stage before cooking several days in advance, and bake them on the day of the party, having first defrosted them. The lollipops

FOOD & SWEETS FOR KIDS

✿ Leaf invitation cookies

✿ Mini hamburgers

✿ Mini hot dogs

✿ Savory pumpkin tartlets

✿ Hard candy apple lollipops

✿ Apple basket cake

✿ Pink marshmallow apples

FOOD & SWEETS FOR MOMMIES AND DADDIES

✿ Mushroom and goat's cheese triangles

✿ Savory pumpkin tartlets

✿ Turkey and mushroom pie

✿ Pumpkin muffins

✿ Little pumpkin cream and hazelnut pies

✿ Spicy autumn apple pie

can be prepared up to a week in advance, and stored between sheets of non-stick paper in a cookie jar, in a dry place. Prepare the marshmallow apples the day before, together with the cake, so that they are fresh and soft. Keep the cake in the refrigerator. The invitation leaves can be prepared well in advance, as gingerbread cookies will keep for a long time in a cookie jar. If you like, before baking them, you can make a hole in the center of each cookie, so that when they are cooked, you can thread a thin ribbon through them. This way, your young guests can keep them until Christmas and use them as tree decorations.

   The children's party favors can be red apple lollipops that will keep them pleasantly busy on their way home. Cover them with plastic wrap, and tie the bottom with a red ribbon.

   At the end of the party, don't hesitate to give the mothers disposable trays filled with pieces of cake, or savory pies or a piece of apple pie, for the next day's morning coffee. Be sure that they will appreciate it, and will soon want to copy you at their own child's party.

Mushroom and Goat's Cheese Triangles

Yields 40 triangles
Preparation time 1 hour
Baking time 30 minutes (200°C/400°F)
<u>Suitable for freezing</u>
Degree of difficulty ☺☺

- 35g (1oz) dried porcini mushrooms
- 1 cup warm water
- 2 tablespoons margarine or butter
- 1 clove garlic, crushed
- 1 cup finely chopped canned mushrooms
- 300g (12oz) creamy goat's cheese
- 2 tablespoons finely chopped parsley
- 2 tablespoons finely chopped
  red jarred peppers
- 1 egg
- 1/2 teaspoon freshly ground black pepper
- 12 Beirut pastry sheets – thin phyllo
  pastry sheets for desserts (450g)
- 1/3 cup olive oil
- some nice sprigs of parsley, mint, or
  heart-shaped pieces of jarred red pepper

1. You can find the thin phyllo sheets in a Greek deli. Soak the porcini mushrooms in water for 15 minutes, until soft. Drain and chop.

2. Melt the butter in a large skillet and sauté the garlic and canned mushrooms until the water evaporates. Add the chopped porcini and stir for a while over heat.

3. Remove from the heat, and when cold, add the cheese, parsley, peppers, egg, salt and pepper, if necessary, and mix. The mixture must be soft, but not runny. Refrigerate the filling for 20 minutes, until thick.

4. Butter the pastry sheets lightly, cut into strips and make triangular mini pies, filling each strip with the cheese mixture. Before folding the triangle for the last time, wrap in a sprig of parsley or mint, or a small heart cut out of well-drained red pepper. At this stage, the triangles can be frozen, covered.

5. Arrange on a baking pan, just before serving, butter the surface and bake at 200°C (400°F) for 25-30 minutes.

Yields 20 mini hot dogs
Preparation time 2 hours
Baking time 30 minutes (200˚C/400˚F)
Degree of difficulty ☺☺

- 20 cocktail Frankfurters,
  wrapped in bacon slices
- ketchup and mustard

for the buns
- 1 cup water
- 1½ cups milk
- 1/4 cup unsalted butter
- 3 tablespoons sugar
- 1 tablespoon salt
- 1 tablespoon dry yeast
- 6-6½ cups plain flour
- 1 egg yolk, beaten with a little oil
- 2 teaspoons sesame seeds

Mini hot-dogs

1. Buy around 20 mini hot dog buns, or make your own at home.

2. Heat the water, milk, butter, sugar and salt in a small saucepan over low heat. Pour the mixture into a large bowl and let stand until it cools. Add and mix in the yeast and let the mixture rise for 10 minutes.

3. Add the flour, a little at a time, and knead the mixture. Make soft and elastic dough that doesn't stick to your hands. Cover and let the dough stand for 3 hours.

4. Divide the dough into 20 small balls and shape into oval buns. Place them on buttered baking trays, leaving some space in between, cover and let rise for 30 minutes. Coat with a little egg yolk and sprinkle with sesame seeds, if you like. Bake the buns at 200˚C (400˚F) for 25-30 minutes. When cold, cut the buns open with a sharp knife and fill them, or store in bags in the freezer.

5. Coat the Frankfurters in a little oil, and sauté them in a large skillet, until the bacon is cooked. Cut the buns open lengthways, season and spread with a little ketchup.

6. Place the warm sausages inside and arrange the mini hot-dogs in an oven dish. Store covered in the refrigerator. Drizzle with a little melted butter and heat for 15 minutes before serving. Garnish with a little mustard from a tube.

Small Pumpkin Cream and Hazelnut Pies

Yields 6 12-cm (5-in) pies
Preparation time 20 minutes
Baking time 45 minutes (180°C/360°F)
Degree of difficulty ☺☺

- 1 recipe sweet pie pastry
  (recipe on page 209)

for the filling
- 3/4 cup sugar
- 2 teaspoons pumpkin pie spice mix
- a pinch of salt
- 3 small eggs
- 1 can (400g/ 16oz) pumpkin pie filling or
  1½ cups blanched pumpkin, drained
- 1¼ cups evaporated milk or buttermilk
- 1 cup coarsely ground hazelnuts

1. Prepare the pastry and roll out six circles, 15 cm (6 in) in diameter. Roll each piece of dough out on a floured pastry cloth. Overturn each circle with the cloth and use it to line a well-buttered small pie pan (12cm/ 5in) with removable bottom. Trim the pastry from around the pan and use it to make a ribbon to stick around the rim of the pie. Press the circumference of the pastry down, to make grooves. Cut leaves or pumpkins out of the remaining pastry, using mini pastry cutters.

2. Mix the sugar and spices, salt and eggs for the filling in a large bowl. Add the pumpkin and milk and mix with a spoon, to obtain a uniform mixture. The mixture must not be beaten or over-stirred. Pour the mixture into the pie molds. Bake at 220°C (425°F) for 20 minutes. At this stage, open the oven and sprinkle the surface of the pies with the hazelnuts. Place two pastry shapes on each pie. Reduce the temperature to 180°C (360°F) and continue baking for another 25-30 minutes, until the cream thickens. Remove the pies from the oven and let cool. Unmold and keep refrigerated. Serve cold, garnished with whipped cream.

Pecan Pumpkin Muffins

Yields 18 muffins or 48 mini muffins
Preparation time 30 minutes
Baking time 40 minutes (175°C/350°F)
Degree of difficulty ☺

- 3 cups self-raising flour
- 1/4 teaspoon bicarbonate of soda
- 1/2 cup caster sugar
- 1/2 cup brown sugar
- 2/3 cup margarine
- 1 cup canned pumpkin pie filling or
  fresh pumpkin, blanched and strained
- 3 eggs
- 1 teaspoon ground cinnamon
- 1/2 teaspoon clove powder
- 1/2 teaspoon ginger powder
- 1/3 cup orange juice or milk
- 1/2 cup coarsely ground pecans and
  1/2 cup chopped sultanas (optional)

1. Mix all the ingredients except the pecans and sultanas in the mixer bowl. Beat for 2 minutes at medium speed. Meanwhile, mix the walnuts and sultanas with 1 tablespoon flour. Stop beating, add and mix into the dough.

2. Pour the dough into muffin trays, lined with paper cupcakes. Bake the muffins at 175°C (350°F) for 40 minutes.

3. When the muffins are cooked, decorate them with orange icing from a tube and black caster sugar. If you like, make small pumpkin muffins (photograph on page 158), coating the surface with orange royal icing. Draw vertical lines on the icing with a toothpick, stick a piece of fig preserve on top for the stalk and sprinkle with orange glittering sugar.

Leaf Invitations

Yields 16 large cookies or 30 smaller ones
Cooking for kids

- 1 recipe gingerbread dough
  (recipe on page 35)

for decorating
- 1 recipe easy royal icing (recipe on page 29)
  colored orange or
  1 tube store-bought orange icing
- autumn leaf paper patterns, diameter 15 cm
  (6 in)

for the invitations
- colored cardboard (autumn colors)
- gelatine paper and ribbons for packaging

1. Copy the leaf pattern onto parchment paper. Cut egg-sized balls of dough and make 5-mm (0.2-in) thick sheets with a rolling pin, on the baking pan used for baking the cookies. Use the pattern to cut leaves out of the dough. Trim off the extra pieces of dough. Repeat, until you have 2 large cookies in each pan.

2. Bake at 190°C (375°F) for 15-20 minutes, until the color darkens slightly, but taking care not to burn them. Remove from the oven, let cool a little and transfer to a special cookie rack. Let the cookies dry for several hours, in a dry place.

3. Prepare the royal icing and use it immediately, as it dries extremely fast. Pipe orange colored icing around the circumference of each cookie. Write each guest's name on a different cookie. Let the icing dry for several hours, before wrapping each cookie in gelatine paper together with the invitation, also cut out of colored cardboard with the autumn leaf pattern.

✱ recipe on page 157

Turkey and Mushroom Pie

Savory Pumpkin Tartlets

Yields 8 portions
Preparation time 1 hour
Baking time 30 minutes (200°C/400°F)
<u>Suitable for freezing</u>
Degree of difficulty ☺☺

- 1/4 cup butter
- 1/2 cup grated onion
- 2 cloves garlic, crushed
- 2½ cups turkey breast fillet, chopped
- 1/4 cup plain flour
- 2 teaspoons Italian herb mix
- 2/3 cup dry white wine
- 2 tablespoons mild mustard
- 1/2 cup cream
- 1 cup canned mushroom slices
- 1 recipe rich pie pastry
  (recipe on page 201)

1. Melt the butter in a large skillet and sauté the onion and garlic. Place the turkey pieces in a plastic bag together with the flour, salt, pepper and herbs, and shake to coat the meat. Add the turkey pieces to the skillet and sauté, stirring over high heat, until the flour turns golden.
2. Douse with the wine. Add the remaining ingredients and let the meat simmer for 30 minutes, stirring occasionally. Remove from the heat and let the filling cool. You can prepare the filling one day in advance and refrigerate it.

3. Make a rectangular sheet with half the pastry, and use it to line the bottom and sides of a well-buttered rectangular pie pan, preferably with removable bottom. Pour in the filling. Make another rectangular sheet on a piece of pastry cloth with the rest of the pastry dough, just large enough to cover the pie pan. Cut apples, leaves or pumpkins out of the sheet with a small pastry cutter. Spread the sheet over the filling, and stick the shapes onto it with water. At this stage, cover and store the pie in the freezer. When you want to serve it, defrost, and bake at 200°C (400°F) for 25-30 minutes.

Yields 15 tartlets
Preparation time 1 hour + 1 hour refrigeration time
Baking time 30-35 minutes (180°C/360°F)
<u>Suitable for freezing (unbaked)</u>
Degree of difficulty ☺☺

for the filling
- 1kg (2lbs) pumpkin pieces or
  2½ cups blanched and mashed pumpkin
  or 1lb canned unflavored pumpkin purée
- 1/3 cup olive oil
- 1 medium onion, grated
- 1 clove garlic, crushed
- 1 teaspoon fresh rosemary
- 1/2 cup semolina
- 250g (8oz) feta cheese, crumbled
- 1/3 cup grated sweet yellow cheese

for the dough
- 1¹/₃ cups olive oil
- 1¹/₃ cups white dry wine or ouzo
- 1½ teaspoons salt
- 5½-6 cups plain flour

1. If you purchase a large pumpkin it is easier to clean if you bake it for 20 minutes in a preheated oven at 200°C (400°F). Cut in half, discard the pips and remove the flesh. Measure the amount you need for this recipe, seal the rest of the pumpkin pieces in a plastic food bag and store in the freezer for future use. Heat the oil in a saucepan, add and sauté the onion and garlic. Add the pumpkin pieces, the rosemary, salt and pepper. Cover and simmer until the pumpkin melts. Add and mix in the semolina and cheeses.
2. Place the oil, wine and salt for the pastry in the mixer bowl. Add 5½ cups flour and knead to obtain soft pliable dough. Add more flour if the dough is too soft. Stand in the refrigerator for 1 hour.
3. Cut egg-sized pieces off the pastry and roll out thick sheets using a small rolling pin. Place a little filling in the center and lift the sides. Pinch them together so that they half-cover the filling. Butter a baking pan and arrange the tartlets on it. At this stage, the tartlets can be stored, covered, in the freezer. Defrost and bake at 180°C (360°F) for 30-35 minutes, until golden brown. Serve warm.

Mini Hamburgers

Yields 20 mini hamburgers
Preparation time 1 hour
Suitable for freezing (unbaked)
Degree of difficulty ☺☺

for the burgers
• 800g (1lb 12oz) veal or lamb or porterhouse ground meat
• 1 large onion, grated
• 1 clove garlic, crushed
• 3 tablespoons dried breadcrumbs or semolina
• 2 tablespoons ketchup
• 2 tablespoons olive oil
• 1 egg
• 1/4 cup grated sweet yellow cheese
• 1 teaspoon Italian herbs
• 1 teaspoon paprika or BBQ seasoning

for garnishing
• 20 store-bought mini brioche or homemade buns or brioche
• 20 slices cheddar cheese for sandwiches
• 10 gherkins, sliced in half lengthways
• 5 small tomatoes, sliced
• ketchup and crisps

1. Place all the hamburger ingredients, salt and pepper in a large bowl, and knead to incorporate. Refrigerate the meat mixture for 15 minutes.

2. Shape the meat mixture into hamburgers, the same size as the buns. At this stage, wrap the burgers in aluminum foil and store them in the freezer.

3. On the day of the party, cook the burgers in a non-stick skillet, without oil, turning them over often to cook on both sides. Reduce the heat a little, so as not to burn them. Remove the burgers to a stainless steel platter. Alternatively, cook them on a grill, 5-7 minutes on each side. Cover with the cheese and cook for another 2-3 minutes, until it melts.

4. Cut the buns in two, season and fry on both sides, until lightly browned. Place a burger and a slice of cheese on each bun bottom. Cover with the tops and press inside the skillet with a spatula, until the cheese melts from the heat. Remove to a platter and serve.

5. If you like, you can wrap the hamburgers in non-stick paper, tied with string on either side, to keep them warm, or to heat easily in an air-heated oven at 200°C (400°F) for 5-6 minutes. When serving, use scissors to cut off half the paper, and expose the hamburger, and serve in plastic cups full of crisps. Accompany with gherkins, which kids love, tomato slices and ketchup.

Spicy Autumn Apple Pie

Yields 8 portions
Preparation time 1 hour
Baking time 50 minutes
<u>Suitable for freezing (unbaked)</u>
Degree of difficulty ☺☺

- 1 recipe pastry dough for sweet pies (recipe on page 209)

for the filling
- 6 cups peeled, cored and chopped apples
- 2 tablespoons lemon juice
- 1 teaspoon lemon zest
- 3/4 cup sugar
- 2 tablespoons cornstarch
- 1 teaspoon ground cinnamon
- 1/4 teaspoon clove powder, nutmeg
- 3 tablespoons melted butter
- 1/2 cup coarsely ground roasted pecans
- 1/4 cup sultanas

1. Roll out a sheet using half the pastry, 5 cm (2in) larger than the pie pan, and use it to line a 23-cm (9-in) non-stick pie pan, covering the bottom and sides.
2. Place the apples in a small saucepan and drizzle with the lemon juice. Add the lemon zest, sugar and cornstarch, stir and simmer over low heat, until the mixture thickens a little. Pour into the pastry-lined pan and sprinkle with the spices. Drizzle with the melted butter and sprinkle with the pecans and sultanas.
3. Make a round sheet on a well-buttered piece of pastry cloth or between two sheets of grease-proof paper, using the other half of the pastry, and cut out a round shape using a large pie pattern with apple designs. Overturn onto the filling, without removing the apple shapes, except 2-3, to let the steam out during baking. At this stage, you may freeze the apple pie. Defrost before baking.
4. Brush the surface with melted butter and sprinkle with cinnamon and sugar. Bake the tart at 200°C (400°F) for 45-50 minutes, until golden brown. Serve slightly warm. If you like, accompany with scoops of vanilla ice cream.

Hard Candy Apple Lollipops

Yields 8 apple lollipops
Preparation time 15 minutes
Refrigeration time 20 minutes
Degree of difficulty ☺☺☺☺

- 2/3 cup water
- 2 cups sugar
- 1/4 teaspoon cream of tartar
- a few drops red food coloring

1. Line a flat oven tray with aluminum foil. Place 8 apple-shaped pastry cutters, diameter 8 cm (3in), next to each other on the foil. If they don't fit, use two trays. Spray the pastry cutters and aluminum foil with oil, or brush them with a little oil. Lift the aluminum foil all around, so that the caramel doesn't spill out, taking care not to make wrinkles in the foil inside the pastry cutters.

2. Place the water, sugar and cream of tartar in a clean, dry, deep non-stick pan. Mix with a wooden spoon over low heat. Stop stirring and let the syrup boil. As soon as it starts to boil, add the food coloring. Do not stir the syrup at all. The caramel will be ready in exactly 12 minutes. If you have a caramel thermometer, stand it in the caramel without it touching the saucepan's bottom, and let it reach 245°C (500°F). Another experiment that will show you if the caramel is ready is to dip a clean dry spoon inside, take a little caramel and drop it into a glass of water. If it forms a hard ball, then the caramel has reached the stage where it will harden to make the lollipops.

3. Remove the saucepan from the heat and pour the caramel into the molds immediately. It doesn't matter if the caramel runs out under the pastry cutters and onto the foil, provided the pastry cutters are about half-full. Refrigerate the tray with the molds and caramel for at least 20 minutes.

4. Remove from the refrigerator and carefully separate the caramel apples from the pastry cutters. Any leftover pieces can be broken off carefully and melted again in a non-stick saucepan. Arrange the caramel apples on a clean flat tray, lined with non-stick paper, and use the leftover melted caramel to attach a lollipop stick to each apple. Let stand in the refrigerator for a further 10 minutes. The lollipops are ready. Will keep for 1 week in a cool dry place. Avoid making lollipops when the weather is hot and humid.

Hot Chocolate and Marshmallows

Yields 6 cups hot chocolate
Preparation time 20 minutes
Degree of difficulty ☺

- 250g (8oz) high quality dark chocolate
- 6 cups milk
- 1/4 cup sugar
- 1/2 teaspoon ground cinnamon
- 1/2 teaspoon vanilla essence
- 1/8 teaspoon clove powder
- a little cocoa or cinnamon for dusting
- chocolate flakes and marshmallows for garnishing

1. Melt the chocolate in a double boiler. Heat the milk but don't let it boil. Pour the melted chocolate into the milk and stir briskly.

2. Add the sugar, cinnamon, vanilla and clove powder and bring to the boil, stirring briskly with a wooden spoon, until foamy.

3. Serve the hot chocolate in large mugs and drop in 1 tablespoon marshmallow cream (recipe follows). For greater ease, instead of marshmallow cream, add whole white marshmallows and sprinkle with chocolate flakes. For adult guests, instead of marshmallows, add 1-2 tablespoons Grand Marnier to the hot chocolate. Sprinkle with cocoa or cinnamon.

Marshmallow Cream – Italian Meringue

Degree of difficulty ☺☺☺

- 1/2 cup water
- 1 cup sugar
- 1/4 teaspoon cream of tartar
- 3 large egg whites

1. Heat the water, sugar and cream of tartar in a small saucepan, over high heat. Stir the mixture until it starts to boil. Let it boil, without stirring, until the caramel thermometer shows 240˚, around 10 minutes.

2. While the syrup is boiling, whisk the egg whites until frothy. Continue beating at low speed, and pour in the syrup, in a constant steady flow. Increase the mixer speed and beat the mixture for another 4 minutes, until it thickens and forms a smooth, shiny meringue that holds stiff peaks.

Sweet Christmas Buns

Yields 10 buns
Preparation time 3 hours
Baking time 25-30 minutes (200°C/400°F)
<u>Suitable for freezing</u>
Degree of difficulty ☺☺☺

- 1 cup boiling milk
- 1/4 cup melted butter
- 1/2 cup sugar
- 1 tablespoon orange zest
- 1 teaspoon vanilla essence
- 1 teaspoon salt
- 1 teaspoon powdered dry yeast
- 1 cup warm water (40°C/75°F)
- 6 cups all-purpose flour
- 1/2 teaspoon bicarbonate of soda
- 1/2 cup brown sugar
- 1 cup black currants or
  finely chopped glacé orange or
  chocolate chips
- 1 egg yolk beaten with a little water
- 10 empty, clean cans

1. Mix the boiling milk with the butter, sugar, orange zest, vanilla and salt. Let the mixture cool a little.

2. Dissolve the yeast in the warm water, add and mix in a little flour, to obtain a thick batter. Let the mixture rise, for about 20 minutes, until double in volume. Sift the rest of the flour with the baking soda into the mixer bowl and make a hole in the center. Pour in the risen yeast and the milk with the other ingredients, and knead for 10 minutes with the dough hook, to obtain smooth and elastic dough.

3. Place the dough in a buttered bowl and brush the surface with a little butter. Cover and stand in a warm place for about 2 hours, until double in volume.

4. Press the dough down to deflate. Divide in half. Roll out two oblong sheets, 30x40cm (30x16 in) and spread over the brown sugar and raisins or glacé orange or chocolate chips. Starting with the longer side, make two rolls. Cut 6-cm (2.5-in) slices with a sharp knife, and knead them into finger buns.

5. Butter 10 empty cans well. If you don't have that many cans, bake the buns in two sets. Press the dough pieces into the cans, to fill 2/3. Cover with plastic wrap and let rise for 20 minutes. Brush the surface with egg yolk whisked with a little water.

6. Bake at 200°C (400°F) for around 25-30 minutes. Remove from the cans and let cool on a rack. If you have trouble removing the buns, let the cans cool and open the bottoms with a can opener. The buns can be stored in the freezer, in plastic bags.

Filled Panettone

At Christmas, food stores are full of delicious Panettone, traditional Christmas sweet bread from Italy. You can buy mini panettone, as many as your party guests, to give to them at the end of the evening. Carefully cut a thin slice off the top, and remove the inside with a sharp knife, without reaching the bottom, and leaving the sides intact. Fill with strawberry and pistachio ice cream or make pink and green cream and use that to fill the mini panettone. Alternatively, make your own buns with currants or glacé orange and bake them in clean empty cans. Wrap in gelatin paper and tie with festive colored ribbons.

Pistachio or Strawberry Cream

- 2 sachets instant pistachio or
  strawberry pudding
- 1 cup milk
- 1 cup whipping cream
- a few drops red or green food coloring

Beat all the ingredients together in the mixer until the cream thickens. Prepare the cream just before using it.

Snowflake Cookies

Yields 20 12-cm (5-in) cookies
Preparation time 1 hour
Baking time 20-25 minutes (200°C/400°F)
Degree of difficulty ☺☺

- 1 recipe butter cookies (recipe on page 35)
- 1 cup royal icing (recipe on page 29)
- silver sugar balls
- snowflake pastry cutters, diameter 12 cm
  (5 in)

1. Prepare the cookie dough. Roll out a 3-mm (paper-thin) pastry sheet on a lightly floured surface, using a rolling pin. Cut snowflake cookies out of the dough using special pastry cutters, and transfer them carefully to an unbuttered baking pan. If you don't have suitable pastry cutters, copy the cookie pattern on the next page onto thin paper and then onto cardboard, to make your own pattern.

2. Arrange the cookies leaving a small distance between them, because they will rise as they bake. Bake on the oven's bottom shelf, at 200°C (400°F) for 20-25 minutes.

3. Remove from the oven and let cool. Prepare the egg icing and use it to fill a piping bag with a pencil-thin nozzle, #5 or 6. Pipe icing around the cookie border. Stick a few silver sugar balls here and there. Let the cookies stand for 2-3 hours, until the icing dries. Will keep for 1 week in a cookie jar.

✴ recipe on page 171

Cookies'n'Cream Cheesecake

Yields 16 portions
Preparation time 20 minutes
Baking time 1 hour (160°C/325°F)
Degree of difficulty ☺☺

for the crumb crust
- 2 cups Oreo cookies with cream, ground (around 16 cookies)
- 1/4 cup unsalted butter

for the filling
- 1kg (2lbs) cream cheese
- 1/2 cup caster sugar
- 1/4 cup plain flour
- 1 teaspoon vanilla essence
- 4 eggs
- 3 egg yolks
- 1/3 cup double cream
- 2 cups coarsely ground Oreo cookies with cream (around 16)
- 1 cup whipping cream, for covering
- 1 tablespoon icing sugar
- a little lemon juice
- a little lemon zest

1. Pulse the ground Oreo cookies with the butter in a food processor. Spread the mixture evenly to cover the bottom of a spring-form pan, diameter 26 cm (10 in). Freeze for 20 minutes.

2. Beat the cream cheese with the sugar, flour and vanilla in the mixer bowl at high speed, until a homogeneous silky mixture is formed. Beat in the eggs and egg yolks one at a time, just until incorporated, scraping the sides of the bowl and the beaters after each addition. Add the double cream and continue beating for a few seconds at low speed.

3. Scrape half the cheese mixture into the pan and sprinkle with half the coarsely ground Oreo cookies. Cover with the other half of the mixture and bake at 200°C (400°F) for 15 minutes. Lower the temperature to 160°C (325°F) and continue baking for another 1 hour, or until the center of the cheesecake is thick and doesn't move if you shake the mold gently. If it is too runny, continue baking until it sets. Switch off the oven and let the cheesecake cool inside it, with the door half-open. When cold, refrigerate for 4 hours in the mold.

4. Whip the cream with the icing sugar and lemon juice until stiff. Add and mix in the lemon zest. Garnish the cheesecake with the aromatic whipped cream, the rest of the coarsely ground cookies and a few frosted maraschino cherries.

Frosted Cherries

Dry a few red or green maraschino cherries on absorbent paper. Whisk 1 egg white lightly in a bowl, just until frothy. Place a little sugar in a second bowl. Dip the cherries one by one into the egg white and then in the caster sugar. Arrange them on a platter lined with non-stick paper until the sugar hardens.

Noël Chicken Roll

Yields 10 portions
Preparation time 30 minutes
Baking time 1 hour (200°C/400°F)
Suitable for freezing (unbaked)
Degree of difficulty ☺☺☺

- 1 chicken (1½kg/ 3lbs), skinned and boned
- 400g (16oz) frozen spinach leaves
- 2 tablespoons butter
- 3 cloves garlic, crushed
- 100g (4oz) breadcrumbs
- 2 tablespoons olive oil
- 50g (2oz) pine nuts
- 1/3 cup sultanas
- 2 jarred red peppers
- 1/4 cup ricotta or cream cheese
- salt, pepper, nutmeg

1. Ask your butcher to clean the chicken carefully, leaving nice large pieces suitable for a roll. Alternatively, use 4 chicken breasts, split lengthways. Arrange the chicken pieces on non-stick oven paper spread over a large piece of cling film. Before arranging the chicken pieces, lay a few pieces of string on the paper, with the ends sticking out. Beat the chicken pieces with a meat hammer, to flatten them, and season.

2. Blanch the spinach, rinse, squeeze the leaves between your palms to remove any excess water, and chop them finely. Melt the butter in a small saucepan and sauté the garlic and breadcrumbs. Add the oil, pine nuts, sultanas and spinach. Stir for a few minutes over heat, until no liquid remains. Remove from heat and let the mixture cool.

3. Cover the chicken fillets with the spinach mixture, and spread over the peppers, split in half lengthways. Mix the cheese with a little salt, white pepper and a pinch of nutmeg, and spread it over the peppers, to form a line. Aided by the paper, lift the chicken fillets and fold them over the cheese, to form a roll. At this stage, tie the roll with the string and wrap it with the paper and the cling film.

4. Keep the roll in the refrigerator for 30 minutes, or in the freezer for up to 1 week. Defrost, remove the cling film and bake at 200°C (400°F) for 50-60 minutes. For greater ease, you might bake the roll, with the paper, in a meat loaf pan. When it is cooked, let the roll stand for 15 minutes before slicing it. Serve in slices and accompany with cherry tomatoes and fresh green salad.

Christmas Tree Quiche Lorraine

Yields 8-10 portions
Preparation time 30 minutes
Baking time 25 minutes for the pie crust
(200°C/400°F), 30 minutes for the quiche
(180°C/360°F)
Suitable for freezing (unbaked)
Degree of difficulty ☺☺

for the pâte brisée dough
- 2½ cups plain flour
- 1 teaspoon salt
- 1 cup (2 sticks) butter, chilled and cut in pieces
- 3-5 tablespoons water

for the filling
- 200g (7oz) bacon rashers
- 1 small onion, grated
- 200g (7oz) grated gruyère cheese
- 3 eggs
- 2/3 cup single cream
- 1/2 cup milk
- a little grated nutmeg
- finely chopped parsley and cherry tomato halves, for decorating
- 1 large Christmas tree-shaped pie pan, with removable bottom

1. Pulse the flour, salt and butter in a food processor until the mixture resembles course meal. Add ice-cold water and beat for 1 minute, until a ball of dough forms.
2. Remove the dough from the mixer bowl and roll out a round sheet on a pastry cloth, using a rolling pin, also dressed in cloth. The sheet should be a little larger than the pie pan you intend to use.

3. Butter the pie pan well and place the dough sheet inside, aided by the cloth. Press the dough down with your fingers, so that it covers the bottom and sides of the pie pan, and trim off any excess pieces of dough. Cut miniature Christmas trees out of the extra dough. Stick them to the pie border with a little water. Prick the pie base thoroughly with a fork and refrigerate it for 20 minutes. Bake at 200°C (400°F) for 25 minutes. Remove from the oven and let cool.
4. Sauté the bacon and onion in a small skillet, until golden. Mix with the cheeses and spread the mixture onto the cooked pie crust. At this stage, the quiche can be frozen, covered, for up to 2 weeks. Beat the eggs with the cream, milk and nutmeg, and pour the mixture over the cheese in the pie pan. Bake the quiche at 180°C (360°F) for 30 minutes. Serve warm or cold. Garnish with finely chopped parsley and cherry tomato halves, making the quiche look like a decorated Christmas tree.

Mini Cheese Puffs

Yields 48 mini puffs
Preparation time 30 minutes
Baking time 30 minutes
(210°C/410°F)
Suitable for freezing (unbaked)
Degree of difficulty ☺

- 600g (1lb 4oz) grated feta cheese
- 1/4 cup melted butter
- a pinch of freshly ground pepper
- 1 egg white (from a small egg)
  beaten with
  3 tablespoons dairy cream
- 500g (1lb) homemade puff pastry
  or two sheets frozen puff pastry
- 1 egg, separated, for coating

1. Mix the cheese with the melted butter and pepper in a large bowl. Add the egg white and cream mixture and stir gently. The mixture must be soft but not runny.

2. Spread one of the pastry sheets on a lightly floured surface and divide it into 8 strips on the long side and 6 strips on the short side with a pizza cutter, without cutting right through, to make 48 5-cm (2-in) squares.

3. Place a spoonful of the filling in the center of each square. Coat the border of each square with a little egg white and stick over the second pastry sheet, pressing down to stick the ends together. Use a sharp knife to cut the pastry sheets and divide the squares.

4. Transfer to an unbuttered baking pan and stand in the refrigerator for 15 minutes. At this stage, you can freeze the cheese puffs in the baking pan and transfer them to food bags when frozen. Keep frozen for up to 1 month. Before baking, brush the puffs with the egg yolk mixed with 1 teaspoon water.

5. Bake the squares without defrosting, at 210°C (410°F) for about 15 minutes, until the pastry rises. Reduce the temperature to 160°C (325°F) and continue baking for another 15 minutes, until the puffs are golden. Serve warm, sprinkled with grated feta cheese, to look like snow. Stick a Santa Claus cocktail stick into each one, so that the kids can pick them up easily.

Christmas Kiwi Garland

Yields 10-12 choux
Preparation time 1 hour
Baking time 1 hour (150°C/300°F)
Degree of difficulty ☺☺☺

- 1 recipe choux dough
  (recipe on page 167)
- 6 kiwis, peeled, sliced and halved
- 1 recipe crème pâtissière
  (recipe on page 77)
- 250g (8oz) whipped cream
- pomegranate seeds for garnishing

for the easy royal icing
- 1 cup icing sugar
- 1 egg white, whisked
- a little vanilla powder

1. Cut out a piece of non-stick oven paper, the size of your baking pan. Trace a 25-cm (10-in) circle on the paper, and use the sheet to cover the pan.

2. Prepare the choux dough and use it to fill a large piping bag with a straight 2-cm (1in) nozzle. Pipe large rosettes around the border of the circle you designed, a small distance from each other, so that when they rise in the oven, they join together.

3. Bake the choux at 220°C (425°F) for 15-20 minutes. Lower the temperature to 150°C (300°F) and let them dry thoroughly, 35-40 minutes. When you take the choux garland out of the oven and it has cooled completely, cut it in half horizontally.

4. Prepare the crème pâtissière and mix it with the whipped cream. Fill the bottom layer of the choux with the mixture, and stick two kiwi slices onto each one. Cover with rosettes of the cream mixture and them with the top choux layer.

5. Prepare the royal icing by mixing the icing sugar with the whisked egg white and a little vanilla powder. If it is too runny, add more icing sugar. If it is too thick, add 1-2 teaspoons milk. Drizzle each choux with 1 tablespoon royal icing and sprinkle with pomegranate seeds. Refrigerate the garland for up to 1 day, uncovered so that the choux don't go soggy.

Two-tone Christmas Tree Cookies

Yields 40 cookies
Preparation time 2 hours
Baking time 15 minutes (190°C/375°F)
Degree of difficulty ☺☺

- 2½ cups plain flour
- 1/2 teaspoon cream of tartar
- 1/2 teaspoon bicarbonate of soda
- a little vanilla powder
- 1/2 cup unsalted butter
- 1/2 cup icing sugar
- 1 egg yolk
- 2 tablespoons milk
- green food coloring

1. Mix all the solid ingredients together. Beat the butter with the sugar until creamy white. Continue beating and add the egg yolk and milk. Add the flour in 3 parts and continue beating with the dough hook, until you obtain a soft pliable dough that doesn't stick to your hands. You may need to add a little more flour. Divide the dough into two parts and color one part green with food coloring. Use your hands to make 15-20 cm (6-8 in) long batons with the green and white dough.
2. Place the batons, alternate colors, on a sheet of non-stick paper. Cover with another sheet of non-stick paper and press down with a rolling pin, to make a single striped sheet of dough. Cut small and large Christmas trees out of the dough sheet, placing the pastry cutters sideways for diagonal stripes, or straight for horizontal stripes. Repeat until you run out of dough. Keep the leftover pieces of dough.
3. When you run out of dough, place the leftovers between two sheets of non-stick paper again and roll out with a rolling pin, to make a two-tone sheet of dough. Cut out more colored trees, small and large. Arrange the cookies on unbuttered baking trays and bake them all together in an air-heated oven at 190°C (375°F) for 10-15 minutes. Remove from the oven and let cool on a cookie rack. Store in a cookie jar, away from humidity.

Snowy Rainbow Cake

Yields 14 portions
Preparation time 30 minutes
Baking time 50 minutes (180°C/360°F)
Suitable for freezing (final stage)
Degree of difficulty ☺

- 3 cups self-raising flour
- 1 teaspoon vanilla essence
- 1 cup margarine or soft butter
- 2 cups sugar
- 5 eggs
- 1/2 cup milk
- green and red food coloring
- 1/4 teaspoon bitter almond essence
- 1/2 teaspoon cinnamon

1. Beat the flour, vanilla, margarine, sugar, eggs and milk together for 4 minutes in the mixer, at high speed. Divide the cake batter into 3 bowls. Color one part green and flavor it with the bitter almond essence. Color the second part red and flavor it with the cinnamon.
2. Butter the baking pan thoroughly and pour in alternate layers of the cake mix. Do not mix the three colors; this will happen as the cake cooks. Bake the cake at 180°C (360°F) for 50 minutes. Remove from the oven and overturn onto a serving platter. Dust with icing sugar and serve with a cup of tea or coffee.

Savory Puffs

Yields 20 puffs
Preparation time 15 minutes
Baking time 15 minutes (200°C/400°F)
Degree of difficulty ☺

- 20 round or square puff pastry pieces
- black and white sesame seeds,
- poppy seeds, caraway seeds, olive slices, small capers, pieces of sun-dried tomato, crispy bacon pieces
- 2 egg yolks mixed with 1 teaspoon water, for coating

1. Select the ingredients you want to use and place them in small bowls. Divide the puff pastry pieces into two unbuttered baking pans. Use pastry cutters to cut out Christmas shapes such as trees, stars, candy sticks etc., dimensions 7-10 cm (2.5-4 in).
2. Brush the surface with a little egg yolk, taking care not to wet the sides that touch the baking pan, otherwise the pastry will not rise. Sprinkle with the savory ingredients. Refrigerate the puffs for 15 minutes, in the baking pans. Bake at 220°C (425°F) for 5 minutes, or until they rise. Will keep for 1 day in the refrigerator. Heat slightly before serving.

Fruit Jelly Candies

Yields 500g (1lb) fruit jellies
Preparation time 20 minutes
Drying time several hours
Degree of difficulty *

- 3 sachets (3 tablespoons) gelatine
- 1½ cups water
- 1½ cups sugar
- 1/2 teaspoon peppermint extract or strawberry essence or lemon essence
- red food coloring
- sugar for coating

1. Dissolve the gelatine in 1/2 cup of the water. Stand for 10 minutes, until the gelatine swells. Boil the rest of the water with the sugar in a small saucepan, stirring constantly, until the sugar dissolves. Add the swollen gelatine, and stir vigorously until it dissolves. Simmer for 5 minutes. Remove from heat, add and mix in the essence and a few drops red food coloring.
2. Pour the mixture into a square or round non-stick baking pan, 22 cm, coated with a little corn oil. Refrigerate for 3-4 hours, until the mixture sets. Overturn onto a work surface sprinkled with plenty of caster sugar, and cut out lozenges, squares, hearts or animals with mini pastry cutters (2 cm/1in). You can use the mixture to fill special petit plastic molds for candies shaped like animals, flowers, stars or dolls. Refrigerate until set and then fold into the sugar. Fold the shapes in white or red caster sugar, covering all sides, and arrange them on a dish lined with non-stick paper. Stand at room temperature for 3-4 hours, uncovered, until dry. Alternatively, use orange juice or any other fruit juice (except pineapple) instead of water, and use only 1/2 cup sugar.

Christmas Tree Ornament Cookies

Yields 30-40 cookies
Preparation time 2 hours
Baking time 25 minutes (180˚C/360˚F)
Drying time 48 hours
Degree of difficulty ☺☺

- 1 recipe basic gingerbread dough (recipe on page 35)
- 1 recipe royal icing (recipe on page 29) for the cookie borders
- Christmas pastry cutters
- 2 jars (450g or 16oz each) ready-made creamy white frosting, for coating the cookies
- colored ribbons

1. Roll out 4-6mm (about 1/5 of an inch) sheets of gingerbread dough on your work surface (non-floured). Cut snowmen, Christmas trees, toy soldiers, Santas, reindeer or any other shape out of the dough, using special pastry cutters, which imprint their shapes on the dough. Using perimetric pastry cutters, cut out stars or fir-trees, and remove smaller trees or stars from the center.
2. Using a drinking straw, make a hole near the top of each cookie, so that you can thread a ribbon through and hang them on the tree. Make quite a large hole, as the cookies will rise as they cook.
3. Use a spatula to transfer the cookies to an unbuttered baking pan, and bake at 180˚C (360˚F) for 20-25 minutes, until the edges are golden brown. Remove from the oven, let cool for a while and transfer to a cookie rack. Let dry for 24 hours, in a dry place.
4. Prepare the royal icing and use it immediately, as it dries very quickly. Pipe white royal icing around the border of the cookies. Let the icing dry for 48 hours, thread ribbons through the holes, and hang them on the tree.
5. To cover the entire cookies, heat the creamy white frosting over low heat or in a microwave oven, until liquid. If you like, divide the frosting into bowls and color it pale green, or pink. Place the cookies on a rack over a baking pan and drizzle with the frosting, using a spoon. Let dry for 48 hours before attempting to hang them on the tree.

Pink Strawberry Punch

Heart Sponge Cakes (for coffee)

Yields 20 glasses
Preparation time 10 minutes
Cooking for kids
Degree of difficulty ☺

- 4 cups pineapple juice
- 6 cups pink grapefruit juice or
  red orange juice or watermelon juice
- 4 cups soda water or Sprite
- a little grenadine for color
- sugar, as much as necessary
- strawberry chunks

1. You will need a punch pitcher or a large regular pitcher. Mix all the ingredients together, adding as much grenadine and sugar as necessary, to obtain a sweet pink drink. Wash and clean a few strawberries, chop them up and add them to the punch. Children love eating the strawberries out of the pitcher.

This particular drink has been established at my daughter's parties as "Kids' Whisky". An imaginative name for a simple drink or healthy dish often encourages children to enjoy it more, as they so often want to imitate us grown-ups.

Yields 20 mini cakes
Preparation time 10 minutes
Baking time 35 minutes (180°C/360°F)
Suitable for freezing (final stage)
Degree of difficulty ☺

- 1 packet ready-made white cake mix
- 1 cup yogurt
- 1/2 cup milk
- 1 egg and 2 egg whites
- 1/3 cup vegetable oil
- 3 tablespoons strawberry syrup
- 1 teaspoon strawberry essence
- 3-4 drops red food coloring

- 1 7-cm (2.5-in) heart-shaped
  pastry cutter
- 1 jelly roll pan

1. Beat all the cake ingredients together at medium speed for 2 minutes. Pour the mixture into a jelly roll pan, buttered and lined with non-stick oven paper, also buttered.
2. Bake the sponge cake at 180°C (360°F) for 35 minutes, or until a skewer comes out dry. Remove from the oven and let stand for 10 minutes inside the pan. Overturn onto non-stick paper and let cool.
3. Use pastry cutters to cut heart shapes out of the sponge cake. Place the miniature cakes into white jumbo muffin cases and serve. Will keep for a long time in the freezer and up to 1 week at room temperature, covered. Can also be served with strawberry or orange-flavored butter (recipe on page 209).

Avgoustinos would like
to suggest a game!

Young Spyros waiting for
his turn to play!

Happy Cecilia at her friend's
party!

I'm not sure I like this clown, says Vivianne...

Yummy! yummy!

I can't blow hard enough, somebody help me please!

Me, me, it's my turn!

Princess, say cheese!

Vanilla Heart Muffins

Yields 18 muffins
Preparation time 20 minutes
Baking time 40 minutes (180°C/360°F)
Suitable for freezing
Degree of difficulty ☺

for the vanilla cake mix
- 3 cups self-raising flour
- 1 cup soft margarine
- 2 cups sugar
- 4 eggs
- 1/2 teaspoon vanilla
- 2/3 cup yogurt

for decorating
- 1 packet sugar hearts with messages
- 1/2 recipe buttercream icing
  (recipe on page 115) or
  450g (1lb) store-bought
  creamy frosting
- pink food coloring

1. Beat all the cake ingredients together in the mixer at high speed for 4 minutes. Divide the mixture into a muffin tray lined with paper baking cups. The tray should not be buttered.

2. Bake the muffins at 180°C (360°F) for 30-35 minutes. Remove from the oven and let stand for 5 minutes before removing from the tray. Overturn onto a rack and let cool completely.

3. Color the buttercream icing with pink food coloring and fill a piping bag. Pipe rosettes onto the muffins and decorate them with sugar candy hearts with little messages on them. Cover with a food bell so they don't dry out. Will keep fresh for up to 3 days. When cool, cover and store in the freezer without the decorations; they will keep for up to 6 months.

Easy solution: Prepare strawberry muffins using store-bought white cake mix. Beat in the mixer at medium speed for 2 minutes, together with 3 egg whites, 2/3 cup milk, 1/3 cup vegetable oil, 1 cup strawberry yogurt and 3 tablespoons strawberry syrup.

Teddy Bears in Love cookies

**Yields 16 teddy bear cookies
(10 cm/ 4 in)**
Preparation time 20 minutes
Baking time 15 minutes (180˚C/360˚F)
Degree of difficulty ☺

- 1 cup unsalted butter
- 200g (7oz) cream cheese
- 2 cups icing sugar
- 2½ teaspoons vanilla essence
- 2 egg yolks
- 4¼-4½ cups plain flour
- red and green food coloring

1. Cream the butter together with the cream cheese and sugar in the mixer. Add the vanilla and egg yolks and beat to incorporate in the mixture.

2. Mix the flour with the vanilla and add it to the mixer bowl. Beat until you obtain soft, elastic dough. Cut two small pieces off the dough, and color one red and the other green with a few drops of the relevant food coloring.

3. Cut pieces off the large piece of dough and roll out each piece using a small rolling pin. Make sheets larger than the pastry cutter you intend to use, and 3mm thick (paper-thin). Cut a teddy bear out of each piece with a 10cm (4in) pastry cutter.

4. Cut small hearts or small round pieces of the red dough to shape into rosebuds, and stick them near the middle of the teddy bear with a little egg white. Make stalks for the rosebuds with the green dough, and stick them, too, onto the cookie. Fold over the teddy bear's hands so that they touch the body, and stick them on with a little egg white.

5. Bake the teddy bear cookies at 180˚C (360˚F) for 15 minutes. Remove to a rack to cool. Will keep fresh for up to 1 week in a cookie jar.

Mocha Heart Muffins

Yields 12 muffins
Preparation time 2 hours
Baking time 30 minutes (180°C/360°F)
<u>Suitable for freezing</u>
Degree of difficulty ☺☺

- 1 recipe chocolate sponge cake
  (see recipe : "Chocolate Mousse Heart
  Cake")
- 2 six-case heart muffin trays

for the mocha cream
- 1/2 cup soft unsalted butter
- 1 cup (250g) cream cheese, softened
- 1/2 cup icing sugar
- 1 sachet (12.5g or 1 tablespoon) instant
  vanilla-flavored cappuccino
- 1 packet (35g or 2½ tablespoons) instant
  vanilla or chocolate pudding
- 1 cup milk
- 1 cup whipping cream

1. Prepare the mocha cream. Beat the butter with the cream cheese, sugar and instant coffee in the mixer until fluffy. Whisk the instant pudding with the milk and cream separately, until thick. Join the two mixtures in a bowl and refrigerate for 15 minutes, to thicken.

2. Prepare the sponge cake and divide it into the buttered and floured muffin trays. Bake the muffins at 180°C (360°F) for 30 minutes.

3. Remove from the oven and overturn onto a rack to cool. Cut in half horizontally with a sharp knife, and join the two halves with the mocha filling. Pipe rosettes of the remaining cream on top of the muffins and garnish with chocolate coffee beans.

Shy Face Cookies

Yields 10 cookies
Preparation time 30 minutes
Baking time 15 minutes (180°C/360°F)
Degree of difficulty ☺

- 1 recipe "teddy bears in love"
  cookie dough, page 195
- a little peach jam or 1 jar lemon custard

1. Make the same cookie dough as for "Teddy Bears in Love" roll out a thin 3-mm (paper-thin) sheet, and cut out 7-cm (2.5-in) circles with a serrated pastry cutter.

2. Use mini pastry cutters to cut crescent-shaped mouths and round eyes out of half the circles. Spread a little egg white on either side of the mouth and sprinkle with red sugar to make the cheeks.

3. Bake the cookies at 180°C (360°F) for 15 minutes. When cold, join one of each with peach jam or lemon cream (recipe on page 144) or store-bought lemon custard.

Palmiers

Yields 20 palmiers
Preparation time 15 minutes
Baking time 15 minutes
Degree of difficulty ☺

- 250g (8oz) puff pastry (one sheet)
- 2/3 cup sugar
- pink and white shiny sugar

1. Roll out the pastry sheet onto a slightly floured surface. Sprinkle the entire sheet with the caster sugar. Start rolling up the sheet on either side, until the two rolls join in the middle to form "binoculars".

2. Cut thin slices off the rolls with a sharp knife, and arrange them on an unbuttered baking pan, lined with non-stick oven paper. Press each slice down to form a pretty heart.

3. Bake the Palmiers at 200°C (400°F) for 15 minutes. Sprinkle with white or pink shiny sugar when cooked.

Katerina with Hara at her party, February 10th

*recipe on page 162

Grandma Hara's Spinach and Leek Hearts

Yields 30 hearts
Preparation time 1 hour
Baking time 30-35 minutes (200°C/400°F)
<u>Suitable for freezing (unbaked)</u>
Degree of difficulty ☺☺

- 2kg (4lbs) fresh spinach
- 5 leeks, only the white parts, finely chopped
- 1/4 cup margarine
- 1/4 cup olive oil
- 1/3 cup evaporated milk
- 500g (1lb) feta cheese, grated
- salt, pepper
- 4 eggs
- 60 round puff pastry pieces
- 5 six-case muffin trays or 2 trays for 12 regular muffins and 1 tray for 6 heart-shaped muffins

1. Wash and clean the spinach. Blanch, drain and squeeze well to remove any excess water. Chop finely with a pair of scissors.

2. Melt the margarine and butter in a large saucepan and sauté the chopped leeks for a few minutes. Add the milk and simmer until the leeks soften, about 10 minutes. Remove from the heat, then fold in the spinach, cheese, salt and pepper. When the mixture cools, blend in the eggs. Stand the stuffing in the refrigerator while you prepare the pastries.

3. Butter the muffin tray cases well. Roll out half the mini pastries with a small rolling pin, on a lightly floured surface, flatten them, and line the muffin trays. Roll out the remaining pastries and cut them into heart shapes with a 7-cm (2.5-in) pastry cutter. Cover the lined muffin tray cases with the stuffing, almost to the rim. Place the heart shapes over the stuffing.

4. At this stage, cover with cling film and store in the freezer for up to 1 month. Defrost before baking. Bake the mini spinach pies at 200°C (400°F) for 30-35 minutes or until the pastry rises and the surface turns golden. In a fan-heated oven, you may bake more than one tray at a time.

Artichoke and Meat Tartlets

Yields 24 tartlets
Preparation time 1 hour
Baking time 40 minutes (200°C/400°F)
Suitable for freezing (unbaked)
Degree of difficulty ☺☺

- 3 tablespoons olive oil
- 1 large onion, finely chopped
- 500g (1lb) ground pork
- 1/3 cup meat stock
- 1/4 cup freshly squeezed lemon juice
- salt and freshly ground black pepper
- 1/2 cup finely chopped fennel or
  1 small finnochio, grated
- 1/2 cup grated yellow cheese
  (kefalotyri or gruyère)
- 2 large eggs, separated
- 24 round pastries
- 1 can artichoke hearts, 400g (16oz)
- 2 muffin trays for 12 regular muffins

for the Béchamel sauce
- 2 tablespoons butter or margarine
- 2 tablespoons flour
- 2 cups milk
- 1 egg
- salt, pepper and a little grated nutmeg

1. Heat the oil in a large saucepan and sauté the onion until soft. Add the ground meat and stir over heat until any liquid evaporates. Add the stock and lemon juice, salt and pepper, and simmer until the meat is almost soft and there is very little sauce left. Remove from the heat, add and mix in the fennel, cheese and egg whites.

2. Flatten the pastries with a rolling pin on a lightly floured surface, and use them to line the well-buttered muffin trays. Rinse the artichoke hearts and drain them thoroughly. Quarter them and arrange them in the tartlets. Pour the meat mixture over the artichokes. At this stage, cover with plastic wrap and store the tartlets in the freezer for up to 1 month.

3. Prepare the Béchamel sauce. Melt the butter in a saucepan and sauté the flour. Add all the milk at once and stir until the sauce boils and thickens. Remove from the heat, let the sauce cool slightly, then add and mix in the egg yolks, egg, salt, pepper and a little nutmeg. Pour over the meat mixture in the tartlets and spread uniformly. Bake the tartlets for 40 minutes at 200°C (400°F).

Mediterranean Quiche

Yields 12 portions
Preparation time 20 minutes
Baking time 40 minutes (200˚C/400˚F)
<u>Suitable for freezing</u>
Degree of difficulty ☺☺

for the rich pie pastry
- 2½ – 2²/₃ cups plain flour
- 1 cup cold butter, in pieces
- 2 egg yolks
- 1 teaspoon lemon zest
- 3-4 tablespoons lemon juice

for the filling
- 3 tablespoons margarine
- 150g (5oz) finely chopped bacon
- 1/2 cup pieces of jarred sun-dried tomatoes (around 10 tomatoes)
- 1 small onion, grated
- 2 cloves garlic, crushed
- 150g (5oz) crumbled feta cheese
- 1/3 cup grated yellow cheese (kefalotyri or gruyère)
- 2 tablespoons capers
- 1/3 cup finely chopped pitted black olives
- 2 medium eggs
- 1/2 cup double cream
- freshly ground pepper

1. Prepare the dough. Place the flour and the cold butter in the mixer bowl and beat until it forms a ball around the dough hook. If the dough is too sticky, add a little more flour. Add the egg yolks and lemon juice and beat to incorporate in the mixture. Form into a ball the dough without kneading it, as it will become too stiff, cover with cling film and refrigerate for 15 minutes.

2. Roll the dough out onto a pastry cloth and form a circle big enough to cover the bottom and sides of a round or heart-shaped 23-cm (9-in) pie pan with a removable bottom.

3. Butter the pan thoroughly and line with the dough. Prick the dough at various points with a fork, so that it doesn't rise in the oven. Bake at 200˚C (400˚F) for 15 minutes. Remove the baked pie crust from the oven and let cool.

4. Melt the margarine in a skillet and sauté the bacon, onion and garlic. Add the sun-dried tomatoes and sauté for a few minutes. Remove from the heat, then blend in the cheese, capers and olives. Whisk the eggs separately with the cream and a little freshly ground pepper, and fold into the mixture with the other ingredients.

5. Pour the mixture onto the cooked pie crust. At this stage, you may cover the quiche and store it in the freezer for up to 2 weeks. Bake the quiche at 200˚C (400˚F) for 35-40 minutes. When you remove the quiche from the oven, let it cool slightly and transfer to a platter, removing the bottom of the pan.

Pink Princess Cake

Yields 30 portions
Preparation time several hours
Baking time 50 minutes for each cake
(175°C/350°F)
Suitable for freezing (final stage)
Degree of difficulty ☺☺☺☺

- 3 recipes perfect chocolate cake
  (recipe on page 23)
- 1 doll mold and 2 round baking pans,
  26 and 22 cm (10 and 9 in)
- 1 recipe chocolate filling
- 1 recipe vanilla cream filling
- 1 cup raspberry jam
- 2 jars (450g or 15oz each) cake icing
- a few drops red food coloring
- 1½kg (3lbs) Regalice (sugar paste)
- 1 tube white icing and 1 tube pink icing
- nozzles for the tubes

1. Prepare the cake mix and divide it into the three baking pans, which should be well buttered and floured. (The doll mold is conical, 24cm/9in in diameter and 20cm/8in high). Bake the cakes separately at 175°C (350°F) for 50 minutes. Remove to a rack and let cool completely. Prepare the cakes one day in advance.

2. Prepare the chocolate and vanilla fillings. Divide the two round cakes into three layers each, and the conical one into 4 layers. Use a knife to make a groove in the center of the cone, to fit in the doll. Remove the legs from a child's mannequin doll, and use only the bust and arms. Wrap the bust and arms in cling film and place the doll in the groove.

3. Place the largest layer directly onto a serving platter. Spread with a little raspberry jam, heated until soft, and then cover with a layer of chocolate filling. Cover with the second layer. Repeat, coating each layer with jam and then chocolate or vanilla filling alternately, ending with the tip of the cone. Stabilize the tall cake by sticking in 2 or 4 long wooden skewers. Fit the mannequin doll into the center of the cake. At this stage, you can cover the cake with cling film and keep it for 1 day in the refrigerator or longer in the freezer.

4. Decorate the doll cake. Heat the icing until runny and mix in a few drops of red food coloring, to make it pink. Let it cool slightly and pour over the cake to cover the whole dress.

5. On a work surface sprinkled with icing sugar, roll out a 3-mm (paper-thin) sheet of Regalice using a rolling pin. Cut out a half-circle piece with a knife, big enough to cover half of the doll's dress. Transfer the piece onto the cake and press down with your hands to stick it onto the icing.

6. Repeat the process with another 1/4 of the Regalice to form the back of the doll's skirt. If the join is not perfect, don't worry, because you can cover it with rosettes made with the icing tube. Cut two pieces off the remaining Regalice for the top halves of the doll's skirt and save a smaller piece for the doll's jacket and the ribbons at the back of the dress. Stick the sleeves and bust of the dress onto the cling film with a little icing. Pipe a few rosettes of white icing onto the front of the bust.

7. Prepare the bows and ribbons by cutting long thin strips off the pink sugar paste. Stick them onto the back of the dress with some water. Decorate the opening of the dress at the front with rosettes of pink and white icing. The cake will keep for up to 2 months in the freezer and 1 week in the refrigerator. Make space in the fridge or freezer before making the cake, as it is quite large.

Chocolate Filling

- 1 packet (35g or 2½ tablespoons) instant
  chocolate pudding
- 2 cups whipping cream
- 2 cups milk
- 1 cup unsalted butter
- 400g (16oz) cream cheese
- 1 teaspoon vanilla extract
- 1/3 cup icing sugar
- 1/3 cup unsweetened cocoa

1. Beat the instant pudding with the cream and 1½ cups milk, until thick. Beat the butter with the cream cheese, the vanilla and icing sugar separately, until soft. Add the remaining milk and the cocoa, and whisk to form a soft cream. Mix the butter cream with the chocolate mixture, to obtain a smooth cream.

Vanilla Cream Filling

- 2 packets (35g or 2½ tablespoons each)
  instant vanilla pudding
- 2 cups whipping cream
- 2 cups milk
- 1 cup unsalted butter
- 400g (16oz) cream cheese, softened
- 1/3 cup icing sugar

1. Beat the instant pudding with the cream and 1½ cups milk, until it forms a thick cream. Beat the butter with the cream cheese and icing sugar separately, until soft and creamy. Add the remaining milk, and whisk the mixture to soften. Join the two creamy mixtures, stirring gently.

Chocolate Heart Cookies with cookies'n'cream ice cream & Gianduja Sandwich Cookies

Yields 20 7-cm (2.5-in)
sandwich cookies or 40 single cookies
Preparation time 1 hour
Baking time 15 minutes (180°C/360°F)
<u>Cooking for kids</u>

- 1 cup unsalted soft butter
- 1 cup icing sugar
- 1/2 cup cornstarch
- 1½ cups self-raising flour
- 1/8 teaspoon bicarbonate of soda
- 1/8 teaspoon salt
- 2½ teaspoons vanilla powder
- 1/2 cup unsweetened cocoa
- 3 tablespoons milk

1. Beat the butter with the sugar until white and creamy. Sift the cornstarch, flour, soda, salt, vanilla powder and cocoa together into the butter mixture. Then add the milk and beat to form soft and elastic dough. Do not over-knead the mixture.

2. Spread the dough between two sheets of non-stick paper and roll it out to a thin sheet. If it is too soft, refrigerate it for a while. You can give the children pieces of dough and small rolling pins, to make their own cookies.

3. Cut heart shapes out of the dough with a 7-cm pastry cutter. Arrange them on a baking pan lined with non-stick paper. Prick the cookie surface with a fork to make a pretty design. Bake at 180°C (360°F) for 15 minutes.

4. Remove the cookies from the oven and let them cool on a rack. When cold, store them in a cookie jar. Prepare cookies'n'cream ice cream, or buy ready-made ice cream, and serve sandwich cookies, joined with 1 tablespoon ice cream. Store the sandwich cookies in the freezer. Remove 5 minutes before serving.

5. Alternatively, prepare white heart cookies, replacing the cocoa with self-raising flour. Join the cookies with gianduja cream, made by heating 1/3 cup double cream, 200g (7oz) chocolate chips and 1/2 cup chocolate hazelnut spread. When the chocolate mixture melts, remove from the heat and let cool. Spread the cream on half the heart cookies, and cover with the other half. Tie with pretty red ribbons and offer them to the kids at the end of the party.

✱ recipe on page 218

Savory Paprika cookies

Cinnamon & Walnut Rolls

Yields 24 cookies
Preparation time 40 minutes
Baking time 10-12 minutes (180˚C/360˚F)
Degree of difficulty ☺☺

- 2 cups cake flour, not self-raising
- 2 cups grated hard yellow cheese
- 1 teaspoon paprika
- 1/2 cup cold unsalted butter or margarine
- 1/3 cup milk

1. Mix the flour with the cheese and paprika in a large bowl. Add the butter in pieces and knead with the dough mixer, until very crumbly.
2. Add the milk and press the dough with your hands, to form a ball. Do not knead the mixture. Cover the dough ball with cling film and let stand for 15 minutes.
3. Cut pieces of dough and roll out thin sheets on a floured surface, using a lightly floured mini rolling pin. Use playing-card shaped pastry cutters to make 6-7 cm (2.5in) cookies with the dough. Arrange carefully on an unbuttered baking pan, and cook for 10-12 minutes at 180˚C (360˚F).

Yields 12 rolls
Preparation time 20 minutes
Baking time 20 minutes (200˚C/400˚F)
Degree of difficulty ☺

- 1 packet ready-made croissant dough
- 3 tablespoons melted butter
- 1/2 cup sultanas, washed, dried and finely chopped
- 1/2 cup coarsely ground walnuts
- 1/4 cup brown sugar plus 2 tablespoons extra
- 2 teaspoons ground cinnamon
- 1 egg yolk, lightly whisked with 1/2 teaspoon water
- white and pink icing

1. Open the packet of dough and join the 6 triangular pieces in pairs, sticking the join with a little water, to make 3 rectangles. Flatten them out with a rolling pin on a lightly floured surface. Coat the surface with a little melted butter.
2. Mix the sultanas with the walnuts, sugar and cinnamon in a bowl. Sprinkle 1/3 of the mixture onto each pastry sheet and roll up the sheets, starting on the short side. Wet the join with some water to stick it together, and turn the rolls so that the join is facing downwards.
3. Cut each roll into 4 slices, about 2 cm (2/3 in) thick. Place one next to the other with the cut sides facing up and down, on a buttered baking pan.
4. Coat with a little egg yolk and sprinkle with some brown sugar. Bake the rolls at 200˚C (400˚F) for 20 minutes, or until golden.
5. Serve warm, or drizzle with white and pink icing when cold.

Mini Lemon Pies

Yields 18 pies
Preparation time 45 minutes
Baking time 20 minutes (200°C/400°F)

- 1 recipe sweet pie pastry
  (recipe on page 209)
- 1/2 cup freshly squeezed lemon juice
- 1¼ cups sugar
- 1/3 cup cornstarch
- 4 egg yolks, lightly whisked
- 3/4 cup boiling water
- 2 teaspoons lemon zest
- 1/4 cup unsalted butter

1. Roll out two 3-mm (1/8-in) sheets of pastry, and cut out round sheets using pastry cutters, big enough to cover the bottom and sides of 24 tartlet molds with removable bottoms, 7.5cm (3in) in diameter. Prick the dough surface with a fork and bake the pastry cases at 200°C (400°F) for 15-20 minutes. Remove from the oven and let cool in the molds.

2. Prepare the cream. Mix the sugar and cornstarch in a saucepan. Add the lemon juice and egg yolks, and whisk the mixture until smooth. Add all the boiling water at once and simmer the cream over medium heat, stirring constantly for 8-10 minutes, until the cream thickens.

3. Remove the cream from the heat, add the lemon zest and butter, and mix well. Divide the cream into the tartlets, cover with cling film and refrigerate for 1-2 hours or overnight. Serve cold, decorated with frosted baby roses or meringue.

Frosted Baby Roses

- 24 baby rosebuds
- 1 egg white, lightly whisked
- 1/3 cup caster sugar

1. Wash the rosebuds thoroughly and dry them on absorbent paper.

2. Use a small paintbrush to coat the flowers with the egg white, taking care not to damage the petals. Sprinkle with the sugar and let stand for 1 hour on non-stick paper, until the sugar hardens.

Meringue Tartlets

- 4 egg whites
- 1/4 teaspoon cream of tartar
- 1/2 cup caster sugar, mixed with a little vanilla powder

1. Beat the egg whites with the cream of tartar in the mixer at high speed, until frothy. Add the sugar little by little while beating, until you obtain a glossy white mixture that holds stiff peaks.

2. Remove the tartlets from their metal cases and arrange them on a cookie tray. Pipe the meringue mixture onto the cream in each tartlet, using a piping bag. If you like, sprinkle the meringue with some orange zest. Bake the tartlets at 175°C (350°F) for 6-8 minutes, until the meringue is golden. Let cool and refrigerate uncovered. Serve cold.

3. Alternatively: instead of lemon cream, prepare 1 recipe Mexican chocolate filling for the tartlets, and garnish with the meringue.

Marshmallow Clouds

Aromatic Tea

Yields 24 clouds
Preparation time 1 hour
<u>Cooking for kids</u>

- 1 cup colored marshmallows
- 1/2 cup white candy melts
- 1 disposable piping bag

1. Place the candy melts in a piping bag, cut the end off with scissors and place in the microwave oven. Heat at medium temperature for 1 minute, until the candy melts. If necessary, heat for another minute.

2. Pipe rosettes of the melted candy onto non-stick paper. Stick on 2-3 marshmallows and cover with another melted candy rosette. Stick a few more marshmallows here and there. Let stand for 1 hour, until the candy sets.

Yields 8 cups tea
Preparation time 10 minutes

- 2 teaspoons light black tea
- 6 cardamom seeds, peeled and pounded
- 1 cinnamon stick
- 3 cloves
- peel of 1 orange
- honey for serving

1. Place the tea, spices and orange peel into a piece of tulle. Tie with a pretty ribbon and dip in a teapot with 1 liter boiling water. Serve the tea with honey or lemon.

2. Another original idea is to serve sachets of store-bought tea, with white stickers explaining the tea variety. Tie pretty bows around the string. Serve the tea with sugar cubes shaped like butterflies and roses, in different colors.

3. Alternatively, use green tea instead of black. Replace the cloves with 1 allspice corn and lemon peel. Also, try light black tea with 1 split vanilla pod.

Shortbread Cookies

Yields 25 large cookies
Preparation time 1 hour
Baking time 30 minutes (150˚C/300˚F)
Degree of difficulty ☺☺

- 2 cups cake flour, not self-raising
- 1 cup (2 sticks) butter, chilled and
  cut in pieces
- 1/2 cup caster sugar
- 1/4 teaspoon salt

1. Place the flour in a large bowl, add the pieces of butter and knead with a dough hook, to obtain crumbly dough. All the flour should join in crumbles with the butter.

2. Add the sugar and salt and knead with the dough hook a while longer, until they are joined to the rest of the mixture. Cover the dough with plastic wrap and stand at room temperature for 15 minutes. Divide the dough into three bowls. Color two parts of the dough, one with a few drops of red food coloring and the other with a few drops of blue food coloring. Leave the third part its natural color.

3. Cut pieces of dough with your hands and knead them lightly into small balls on a floured surface. The heat from your hands will make the dough join better. Roll the balls out into 3mm (1/8 in) thick sheets using a lightly buttered mini rolling pin. The sheet should not be too thin. Using a serrated pastry cutter, cut out hearts, circles, or any other shape from the pastry sheets. Lift carefully with your hands and place the shapes on a non-buttered baking pan.

4. Bake the cookies at 150˚C, for 25-30 minutes. The cookies should not turn golden-brown. Remove from the oven, and while still soft, remove them carefully from the pan, using a spatula, and transfer them to a rack to cool.

5. Once cold, tie one of each color together with colored ribbons and offer them to the children.

Honey and Shiny Sugar Donuts

Yields 30 mini donuts
Preparation time 1 hour
Frying time 20 minutes
<u>Suitable for freezing</u>
Degree of difficulty ☺☺

- 2 cups cake flour, not self-raising
- 1/2 cup sugar
- 1½ teaspoons baking powder
- a pinch of salt
- 1/4 teaspoon ground cinnamon
- 1 tablespoon melted butter
- 1 egg
- 1/3 cup milk

for garnishing
- 1/4 cup warm honey
- shiny sugar in various pale colors

1. Beat half the flour with the other ingredients for 2 minutes in the mixer, at medium speed, to form thick, lumpy dough. Add the remaining flour and beat to incorporate. The dough should be quite thick and slightly sticky.

2. Dip your hands in flour and form walnut-sized balls of the dough. Press to flatten and use an apple corer to make a hole in the center. Dip the utensil and your hands in flour each time you shape a new donut.

3. Prepare all the donuts and arrange them on non-stick paper before frying them. At this stage, cover and store in the freezer. Deep fry the donuts in heated oil a few at a time.

4. At the beginning, the donuts will sink to the bottom; they will rise to the surface as they cook, however. Turn them over to cook on both sides, until golden-colored. Remove with a slotted spatula onto absorbent paper, to drain off most of the oil.

5. Transfer the donuts to a cookie rack. Drizzle with the warm honey. Stand for 5 minutes until the honey is absorbed, and sprinkle with colored shiny sugar. You may wrap each one separately in gelatine paper and give them to the kids at the end of the party.

Yields 12 cakes, 5x5x5cm (2x2x2 in)
Preparation time 2 hours
Baking time 35 minutes (175˚C/350˚F)
<u>Suitable for freezing</u>
Degree of difficulty ☺☺☺☺

• 1 recipe vanilla sponge cake
  (recipe on page 51)

for decorating
• 250g (8oz) strawberry or cherry jam
• 1 recipe vanilla icing
  (recipe on page 29) or
  450g (1lb) store-bought white icing
• 1 packet Regalice
• food coloring

1. Prepare one recipe vanilla or chocolate sponge cake and bake it in a 25x25 cm (10x10 in) square baking pan. Remove from the oven and overturn onto a cloth dusted with icing sugar and let cool. Cut into five parallel strips and again into five vertical strips, to make 25 miniature square cakes. Make sandwiches with the cake pieces, joining them with a thick layer of jam. There will be one piece left over. Cut it in half and join the two halves with some jam.
2. Divide the Regalice into 3 parts and color one part turquoise with 2 drops blue and 1 drop yellow food coloring. Color the second part pale pink with 1-2 drops red coloring and the third part blue with 1 drop blue coloring.
3. Place the mini cakes on a rack and pour over the icing, to cover all sides.
4. Cut pieces of the colored Regalice that you want to use for "dressing" the cakes, and roll out square 15x15 cm (6x6 in) sheets with a rolling pin on a surface sprinkled with icing sugar. Transfer each sheet carefully onto the cake, while the icing is still soft, and press carefully with your hands, to cover the cake smoothly. Cut the corners off carefully with scissors, and trim the bottom with a knife. Cover all the mini cakes in the same way.

Decorating ideas: Cut a smaller square piece of different colored Regalice and cut out hearts, triangles or clovers with mini pastry cutters. Dot the surface of a small cake with water and stick on the smaller piece of sugar paste. Decorate with designs made with a tube of white icing. To make a gift-cake, cut thin ribbons of white paste and stick them onto a pink cake with water, to make it look like a bow (photograph on page 211). A simpler idea is to cut large hearts out of white or pink sugar paste and stick them onto the cakes with a little water. Dot the hearts with more water and sprinkle with shiny sugar.

Sugar molds

Vanilla Boules

Preparation time 2 hours
Degree of difficulty ☺

- 2 cups caster sugar
- 1/8 teaspoon red food coloring paste
- 2 drops strawberry essence
- 1-1½ teaspoons cold water

1. Place the sugar in a bowl. Add the coloring paste using a toothpick and mix initially with a spoon, to distribute it evenly. Knead the sugar with your hands to color it uniformly. Add the essence dissolved in the water, and then knead the mixture with your hands, to give it a sandy texture.

2. Take pieces of the mixture with your hands and place them into special sugar molds. Let the sugar stand in the molds for 5 minutes, and overturn the shapes onto a plate spread with parchment paper. Set aside the sugar shapes at room temperature, uncovered, for 1-2 hours, until they harden. The longer they stand, the harder they get.

3. Make pink butterflies and roses and flavor them with strawberry essence. Make green leaves or blue teacups and flavor them with peppermint essence. Make yellow suns or shells and scent them with lemon essence. Make orange fruit and flavor them with orange essence. The fruity tastes are perfect with a cup of tea.

Yields 48 mini cakes
Preparation time 20 minutes
Baking time 45 minutes (180˚C/360˚F)
<u>Suitable for freezing</u>
Degree of difficulty ☺☺

- 1 recipe vanilla cake (recipe on page 89) or 1 box vanilla cake mix
- 1 recipe shiny strawberry icing (recipe on page 29)
- hundreds-and-thousands and sugar for decorating

1. Prepare the cake dough, following the recipe or the instructions on the packet.

2. Butter four 12-muffin trays tho-roughly. Spoon the dough into the mini muffin cases, filling 2/3 and taking care not to smear the rims, otherwise the cakes will stick while cooking. Bake at 180˚C (360˚F) for 35-40 minutes.

3. Remove from the oven and overturn onto a rack to cool. Heat the icing until soft, and spoon it over the mini cakes. While the icing is still soft, sprinkle the cakes with hundreds-and-thousands. The cakes can be prepared several days in advance and stored un-garnished in the freezer. Decorate one day before the party.

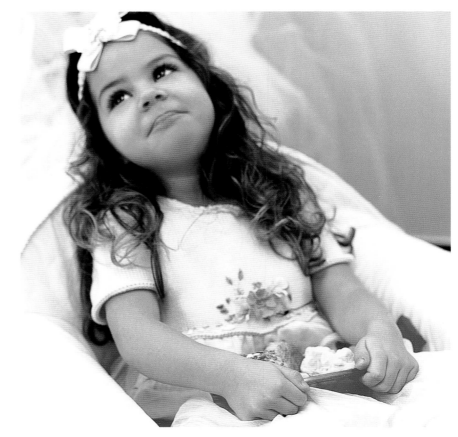

The Blackbird: Savory Pie

Yields 16 portions
Preparation time 30 minutes
Baking time 40 minutes (180°C/360°F)
Degree of difficulty ☺☺

- 1 spring-form pan, 36cm (13in)
- 3 long thin Spuntinelle bread slices or
  10 sandwich bread slices, no crust
- 3 packets refrigerator pizza dough or
  2 recipes homemade pizza dough
- 1/4 cup ketchup
- 2 tablespoons mustard
- 250g (8oz) smoked mozzarella, in thin slices
- 1/2 cup canned sliced mushrooms
- 250g (8oz) Milan salami
- 250g (8oz) sandwich cheese slices
- 1 cup pitted and sliced black olives
- 400g (16oz) jarred red peppers (pimientos)
- 1 jar black sesame seeds
- 1 blackbird paper pattern

1. Butter a spring-form mold thoroughly. Cut the homemade pizza dough into three pieces and roll them out into 26-cm (10-in) circles, using a rolling pin. Spread one sheet on the bottom of the mold. Alternatively, line the bottom of the mold with a round sheet of refrigerator pizza dough. Cut each long thin slice of Spuntinelle bread in half lengthways, and place the pieces around the sides of the mold. Alternatively, cover the sides of the mold with sandwich bread slices, crusts removed.

2. Mix the ketchup with the mustard and spread half of the mixture on the pizza base. Then add layers of the filling ingredients: half the smoked mozzarella, the mushrooms, the salami and end with the rest of the mozzarella. Cover with the second dough sheet. Spread over the remaining sauce and then layers of the other ingredients: half the yellow cheese slices, the olives, the peppers, and end with the other half of the cheese slices.

3. Cover with the last dough sheet. Bake the savory cake at 180°C (360°F) for 35-40 minutes. Remove from the oven and let stand for 15 minutes. Place the cardboard pattern on top of the cake. Coat the bird shape with a little egg white mixed with 1 teaspoon water and sprinkle the shape with black sesame seeds. Carefully remove the pattern, leaving the design on the cake. Open the clasp, remove the ring, and transfer the cake to a serving platter. Serve immediately or store covered in the refrigerator and re-heat before serving.

Yields 6 sandwiches
Preparation time 3 hours
Baking time 25 minutes (180°C/360°F)
Suitable for freezing
Degree of difficulty ☺☺

for the dough
- 3½ cups plain flour
- 1 teaspoon salt
- 1 teaspoon dried yeast
- 1 teaspoon crumbled dried rosemary and oregano
- 2 tablespoons honey
- 1/4 cup olive oil
- 1 cup warm boiled pumpkin purée
- 1/2 – 2/3 cup pumpkin stock

for the filling
- 6 slices turkey ham
- 6 thin cheese slices
- 1/3 cup mayonnaise mixed with
  2 teaspoons mustard
- 6 thin tomato slices

Pumpkin Bread Sandwiches

1. Mix the flour, salt, yeast and dry herbs in a bowl. Add the honey, oil, pumpkin purée and stock. Do not add all the stock at once; use a little at a time, because you may not need it all. If you don't boil the pumpkin fresh, substitute it with canned pumpkin purée and the stock with water. Beat the ingredients with the dough hook, or knead with your hands for 10 or 20 minutes respectively, until you obtain soft, elastic dough that doesn't stick to your hands.
2. Cover and let the dough stand for 2 hours, until double in volume. Press down to deflate and cut off egg-sized balls. Place the balls into pumpkin-shaped molds, coated with oil. Cover and let rise for 20 minutes. Bake at 180°C (360°F) for 25 minutes, or until the surface is golden brown.
3. Remove from the molds and let cool. At this stage store in plastic bags in the freezer. To serve, cut the buns in half, spread with a little mustard and mayonnaise and fill with turkey ham, slices of cheese and tomato. Tie with pretty colored ribbon to serve to your young guests.

Floss Caramel Cakes

Yields 9 cakes
Preparation time 15 minutes
Baking time 30 minutes (180°C/360°F)
Degree of difficulty ☺☺

- 200g (7oz) butterscotch caramel chips
- 1/2 cup caster sugar
- 1/2 cup brown sugar
- 1 cup soft butter
- 2/3 cup evaporated milk
- 4 medium eggs
- 2¹/₃ cups all-purpose flour
- 1 tablespoon baking powder
- a little salt
- 1/2 teaspoon ground cinnamon
- 1/2 teaspoon clove powder
- 1/2 teaspoon bicarbonate of soda
- 1 teaspoon vanilla essence

1. Place the caramel chips, sugar and butter in a large saucepan and melt over high heat, stirring constantly so that the caramel doesn't stick to the pan. Remove from the heat and pour the melted caramel into the mixer bowl. When the caramel cools a little, without setting, pour and mix in the milk. Add the eggs and whisk for 1 minute.

2. Mix the flour, baking powder, salt, spices and soda in a large bowl. Add the flour mixture to the mixer bowl one spoonful at a time and beat to incorporate in the other ingredients. The whole process should take 2 minutes. The mixture will be soft, but not too thick.

3. Divide the dough into well-buttered fancy ring molds, and bake at 180°C (360°F) for 30 minutes. If you like, pour the mixture into a large cake mold, well-buttered and floured. This will need baking for 45-50 minutes. Overturn the cakes onto a rack as soon as you take them out of the oven, to cool.

4. Prepare the caramel as in the 'Hard Candy' recipe on page 162. Prepare half the recipe, without coloring it, and use two forks to make thin threads of caramel over the cakes. Serve within a few hours or keep the decorated cakes in a dry place.

Let's Dip

Make delicious dip-type sauces. Serve these savory and spicy dips with vegetable sticks, such as cucumber or carrot, pepper triangles and various nachos and savory cookies, for lots of 'dipping' fun!

Taco Mexican Dip (...for kids)

- 300g (12oz) cream cheese, softened
- 200g (7oz) sour cream or yogurt mixed with 2 tablespoons lemon juice
- 2 tablespoons taco seasoning
- 1/2 cup finely chopped black and green stuffed olives
- 1½ cups grated yellow cheddar cheese
- 1 teaspoon paprika
- 2 tablespoons ketchup

1. Beat the cream cheese with the sour cream in the mixer until fluffy. Add the remaining ingredients, salt and pepper, and beat to incorporate. Serve cold.

Pesto Dip (...for kids)

- 300g (12oz) cream cheese, softened
- 2/3 ready-made pesto sauce
- 2 tablespoons lemon juice
- 1/2 cup pitted and sliced black olives
- 1/2 cup finely chopped green and red pepper

1. Mix all the ingredients together. Season and serve the dip cold, in small bowls.

Chili Dip (...for kids)

- 1 cup strained yogurt or sour cream
- 1 cup mayonnaise
- 1 tablespoon horseradish sauce
- 1/4 cup chili sauce (store-bought)
- 1/2 cup finely chopped red pepper
- 1/4 cup finely chopped green onion

1. Mix all the ingredients together. Season and serve the dip cold, in small bowls.

Prawn Cocktail Dip (...for adults)

- 200g (7oz) cream cheese, softened
- 1/4 cup mustard
- 1/4 cup ketchup
- 1/2 cup mayonnaise
- 3 tablespoons finely chopped onion
- 1 tablespoon horseradish sauce
- 2 cups cocktail prawns (pre-boiled)

1. Mix the cream cheese with the mustard, ketchup, mayonnaise, onion, horseradish, salt and a little pepper. Add the prawns and keep refrigerated until serving.

Warm Artichoke and Cheese Dip (...for adults, too)

- 2/3 cup mayonnaise
- 300g (12oz) cream cheese, softened
- 1 cup grated cheddar cheese or other soft, sweet yellow cheese
- 400g (16oz) canned artichoke hearts, drained and cut in half
- 20-30 drops Tabasco sauce (optional)
- 1/2 teaspoon onion powder
- 1/4 teaspoon garlic powder
- 1/4 cup finely chopped green onion
- 1/4 cup finely chopped tomato

1. Mix all the ingredients, except the green onion and tomato, in a deep oven dish. Bake at 180°C (360°F) for 15 minutes, until the cheese melts. Season to taste. Serve the dip warm, sprinkled with chopped onion and tomato. Omit the Tabasco sauce for younger guests.

Cocktail Dip (...for kids)

- 1/2 cup mayonnaise
- 1/4 cup ketchup
- 2 tablespoons mustard
- 2 tablespoons BBQ sauce

1. Mix all the ingredients together and stand in the refrigerator for 30 minutes. Serve the sauce with the chicken nuggets.

Spooky Nuggets

Yields 20 chicken nuggets
Preparation time 1 hour
<u>Suitable for freezing (uncooked)</u>

- breast of 2 chickens, skinned, boned, and chopped
- 6 slices ham, finely chopped
- 2 slices bacon, finely chopped
- 2 tablespoons mustard
- 2 cloves garlic, crushed
- salt, pepper
- 1 cup grated soft Gouda, Emmenthal or other tasty yellow cheese
- 2 eggs
- 2 tablespoons olive oil
- flour and breadcrumbs

1. Grind the chicken in a meat grinder. Mix with the ham, bacon, mustard, garlic, cheese, salt and pepper. Refrigerate the mixture until stiff. Shape the mixture into small nuggets. Coat them first with the flour, then dip in egg, beaten with 2 tablespoons oil, and finally coat with the breadcrumbs. Arrange the nuggets on a baking pan lined with parchment paper and freeze until stiff. At this stage, the nuggets can be stored in plastic food bags in the freezer.

2. Before serving, deep fry the frozen nuggets in hot oil. Serve with mustard, ketchup, BBQ sauce or cocktail dip, boiled broccoli and carrots sautéed in 2 tablespoons butter or raw celery sticks. To encourage the kids to eat their vegetables, make small cardboard labels to put on the plate, with a drawing of an alien with broccoli, carrots or celery for hair, and the inscription "Alien Broccoli", "Extraterrestrial Carrots" or "Spooky Celery".

Natalie and her two best friends at her party, October 31st.

The Good Witch:
Chocolate Truffle Cake

Yields 16 portions
Preparation time 1 hour 30 minutes
Refrigeration time 4 hours
Degree of difficulty ☺☺

for the sponge cake
- 1 recipe Devil's food cake
  (recipe on page 23)

for the chocolate mousse filling
- 1 tablespoon gelatine powder
- 1/3 cup milk
- 1/2 cup (1 stick) butter
- 1/2 cup unsweetened cocoa
- 250g (8oz) top quality dark chocolate, cut in pieces
- 2 tablespoons Kahlua
- 2 egg whites
- 1/3 cup caster sugar
- 1 cup whipping cream

for the icing
- 200g dark chocolate
- 1/2 cup (1 stick) butter or margarine
- 4 cups icing sugar
- 1/3 – 1/2 cup warm milk
- chocolate sprinkles for decorating

1. Prepare the cake mix or use ready-made cake mix from a packet. Divide the dough into three round baking pans, diameter 25 cm (10 in), lined with greased oven paper. Bake the sponge cake layers at 180°C (360°F) for about 30 minutes. When they are cold, overturn them onto parchment paper sprinkled with icing sugar. Place one of the layers onto a serving platter and surround with a clasp ring.

2. Prepare the filling. Dissolve the gelatine in the milk and let it swell. Melt the butter in a small saucepan and mix with the cocoa. Add the gelatine and mix until it dissolves. Add the chocolate and stir until it melts. Remove from the heat, add and mix in the liqueur and let the mixture cool. Whisk the egg whites and sugar to a soft meringue. Beat the cream until thick. Fold the chocolate mixture gently into the whipped cream and then into the meringue.

3. Pour half the chocolate mixture over the cake layer in the ring. Cover with the second sponge cake and spread with another layer of chocolate filling. End with the third cake layer and refrigerate for 4-5 hours. Take out of the refrigerator, remove the ring, and coat the cake's sides with chocolate icing and chocolate sprinkles. Place a witch pattern over the top of the cake, and sprinkle with icing sugar. Remove the pattern carefully, to leave the witch design on the cake surface.

4. Prepare the icing. Melt the chocolate and butter over low heat. Remove from the heat and stir in the sugar, essence and as much milk as necessary, to achieve the desired consistency.

Index

(A)

Almonds, roasted 59
American dream salad 99
Angel food cake 23
    ballerina birthday cake 69
    chocolate 69
Apple pies 135
Apple
    basket cake 63
    caramel 43
    lollipops 162
    marshmallows 163
    pie 161
    spicy muffins 42
Applesauce muffins 17
Aromatic butter
    for meat 101
    with liquor 209
    with orange 209
    with strawberry 209
Aromatic tea 215
Avocado dip 103

(B)

Bagels 133
Ballerina
    cake 69
    lollipops 69
Banana beetle cake 125
    sweet bread 143
Béchamel 200
Birthday cakes
    ballerina 234
    ballet 69
    beetle car 125
    blue dream 57
    bunny 234
    butterfly with strawberry sauce and
    whipped cream 83
    carousel with horses 77, 91
    chocolate mousse roll 168
    dream butterfly 78
    duck-pond 144
    footballer 130
    gift-cakes 218
    hamburger 137
    heart with chocolate mousse 65
    lemon delight 179
    marshmallow bunny 127
    maypole 115
    painting 27
    pink princess 203
    Santa Claus 179
    savory Mexican with cheese 105
    siren 149
    stars 'n' spangles 107
    teddy bear cookie 70
    the wicked witch 235

    vegetable garden 121
Blondies 66
Bomb
    chocolate ice cream with meringues 190
    sandwich 117
    sandwich, savory 224
    sandwich, sweet 224
    sandwich, with chocolate spread 224
    three-tone ice cream 116
Bread, guitar brioche 125
Bread, sweet
    banana and cashew nut 143
    chocolate 119
    fruit 143
    lemon and poppy seed 143
    mold 171
    strawberry 143
Brownies
    chocolate with hazelnut 71
    chocolate with pumpkin 121
    Dalmatian 65
    fudgy 66
    mocha 66
    soft 66
    teddy bear 65
Buns 155
    brioche 113
    hamburger 155
    hot dog 155
    pumpkin 226
    sandwich dough 58
Burgers
    chicken 188
    fish 141
    lamb's meat 160
    mini 160
    pork 160
    porterhouse 160
Butterfly
    cake 78
    choux with cream 81
    cookies 36, 89
    jumbo muffins 89
    mini sandwiches 85
    muffins 79
    rosettes 82
    three-tiered cake arrangement 85
    tostadas 85

(C)

Cake
    angel 21
    apple basket 163
    banana 125
    banana and cashew nut 143
    banana, without animal fat 143
    cheesecake with orange 46
    chiffon, with almond and choco
    chips 40
    cookies and cream cheesecake 173

Devil food 23
doll 25
dough with egg whites 89
Hara's strawberry 25
lemon and poppy seed 143
lemon chiffon 144
mocha, with cream filling 44
perfect chocolate 23
pink lemonade 47
salami 119
strawberry 143
tart with cream cheese and
    raspberries 232
vanilla cheesecake 17
Candy, fruit 183
Caramel
    apples with 43
    muffins with 227
Carousel cake 77
Chantilly 77
Cheese pies, mushroom and goat's cheese 154
Cheesecake
    cookies 'n' cream 173
    ice cream with strawberries 109
    marbled 17
    orange 46
    pie with cream and raspberries 231
    vanilla 17
Cherries, sugared 173
Chicken
    croquettes 229
    love burgers 188
    nuggets 229
    roll 174
    tartlets 87
    with peppers in pastry 86
Chiffon cake 144
    with almonds and choco chips 40
Chips, oven 105
Choco armenoville 190
Choco-chip muffins 19
Chocolate
    brownies with hazelnuts 71
    cookies 35
    filling 203
    fudge sauce 21
    Ganache icing 29
    hot drink 169
    ice cream 109
    log cake 235
    muffins 19, 221
    on order 68
    roll with mousse 168
    shakes 53
    shiny icing 71
    soft icing 179, 233
    sponge cake 65, 197, 233
    truffle cake 233
    white mousse 205
Choux
    butterflies with cream 81

dough 167
garland 181
Christmas tree
mini sandwiches 178
two-tone cookies 183
Clouds, marshmallow 215
Club sandwich 132
Coffee cake 210
Coleslaw 132
Coney island hot dogs 98
Cookies
animal 32
butter 35
butterfly 89
chocolate 35
chocolate heart 204
chocolate spread sandwich 204
filled sandwich 204
filled with ice cream 204
heart 63
honeyed 167
leaves 157
peanut butter 109
petit fours with almonds and jam 127
pinwheel 55
savory with paprika 212
shortbread 216
shy faces 197
snowflake 171, 185
snowman 185
spritz 37
sugar 89
teddy bears in love 195
tree decorations 185
two-tone butterflies 36
two-tone trees 183
vanilla, filled 55
Cookies 'n' cream
cheesecake 173
cookies with ice cream 204
ice cream 109
Cookies, Vefa's Easter 167
Crazy for chocolate angel food cake 69
Cream
fruit 209
lemon 144
marshmallow 169
mocha 197
patisserie 77
pistachio 171
strawberry 171
whipped 77
Crêpes
dough for 95
with ham and cheese 95
Croissants
apple 135
cheese 135
Croquettes
chicken 229
fish 141

potato 52
Currant buns 171
Custard, tart with figs and 147

(D)
Daphne's doll's cake 25
Devil's food cake 23
Dip
artichoke, warm with cheese 229
avocado 103
chili 229
pesto 229
prawn cocktail 229
taco Mexican 229
various 229
Donuts with honey and sugar 217
Dough
basic gingerbread 35
bread, for sandwiches 57
bread, with pumpkin 226
cookie, for the fridge 31
for brioche bread 113
for crisp pizza 61
for savory pies 175
for sweet pies 209
for sweet pizza 59
pâte brisée 175
pie pastry, with egg 201
pie pastry, with oil 123
pie pastry, with wine 159
Dream roll with strawberries 106

(E)
Easy
asparagus quiche 145
bunny cake 127
margarita pizza 119
relish 98
soufflé pizza 113
Eggs, teddy bear 52

(F)
Farfalle with pepperoni 87
Filled panettone 171
Filling for cakes
chocolate 203
chocolate and cream cheese 21
chocolate mousse 168, 233
fruit cream 209
lemon 144
Mexican chocolate 27
mocha 197
strawberries and cream 83
truffle 233
truffle mousse 65
vanilla 203
vanilla cream 129
white chocolate 57
Fishburgers 141

Frosted
baby roses 213
cherries 173
Fruit candy 183
Fruit, marzipan 221
Fudge, chocolate 21
Fudgy brownies 66

(G)
Ganache 27
Gianduja, cookies with cream 204
Gingerbread dough 35
Guacamole 103

(H)
Hamburgers 160
Hard candy 52
Hash browns 50
Hats, party 75, 76, 88, 90
Heart cake with chocolate mousse 65
Hearts
lollipop 198
meringue, with whipped cream 205
mini pizzas 189
mini sandwich 189
mocha muffins 197
palmiers 197
pink muffins 191
spinach 199
Honeyed, Vefa's cookies 167
Hot chocolate with marshmallow cream 169
Hot dogs 98
mini 155
relish for 95, 103

(I)
Ice cream
cheesecake with strawberries 109
chocolate 109
chocolate bomb 190
muffins 101
oreo cookie 109
three-tone 116
vanilla 109
Icepops 89
Icing
blue 57
buttercream 115
chocolate ganache 29
chocolate, soft 233
colored fondant 55
easy lemon 29
easy orange 29
easy royal 181
easy vanilla 29
green 121
pink 69
regalice 113

royal 167
shiny chocolate 71
shiny strawberry 29
shiny vanilla 29
soft chocolate 179
soft vanilla 179
Invitations
ideas for 8, 48, 74, 109, 152, 186, 196
leaves 157
Italian meringue 169

(J)
Jumbo butterfly muffins 89

(L)
Lady apples 43
Lemon
chiffon cake 144
cream 144
easy icing 29
sweet bread 143
tartlets with cream 213
Lemonade
with raspberries 46
with strawberry 46
Lollipops
apples 162
ballerinas 69
bunnies 234
footballs 135
hearts 198
roses 127
shamrock 135
various for parties 207

(M)
Macaroni 'n' cheese 97
Marshmallows 51
chocolate with 68
clouds 215
cream 169
hot chocolate with cream 169
pink apples 163
Marzipan 209
fruit 221
Mediterranean quiche 201
Meringue 204
hearts with whipped cream 204
Meringues, pink or blue 77, 190, 205
Milkshake, vanilla 55
banana 55
chocolate 53
Millefeuille, savory 177
Mini
bagels 133
birthday cakes 218
cheese puffs 176
cheesecakes 46